The Symphony ~ 1720–1840

Series A ~ Volume II

Giovanni Battista Sammartini ~ Ten Symphonies

GIO. BATTISTA S. MARTINO MILANESE

MORI L'ANNO 1775 17 GENN. D'ANNI 74

Oil portrait of Giovanni Battista Sammartini, copy after a lost original by Domenico Riccardi, 1778.
The Milanese theorist Giovenale Sacchi (1726–1789) described the portrait as a very good likeness;
the date of death is incorrectly given as 17, instead of 15, January.
(*Bologna, Civico Museo Bibliografico Musicale*)

The Symphony
1720-1840

A comprehensive collection of full scores
in sixty volumes

Barry S. Brook

EDITOR–IN–CHIEF

Barbara B. Heyman
ASSOCIATE EDITOR

A Garland Series

Contents of Collection

Series A ∾ Volume II

Giovanni Battista Sammartini

1700 or 1701–1775

Ten Symphonies

J-C 7, J-C 38, J-C 39, J-C 44, J-C 57, J-C 46,
J-C 4, J-C 62, J-C 52, J-C 26

Edited by
Bathia Churgin

Garland Publishing, Inc.
New York & London   1984

Library of Congress Cataloging in Publication Data

Sammartini, Giovanni Battista, 1700 (*ca.*)–1775.
    [Symphonies. Selections]
    Ten symphonies.

    (The Symphony. Series A ; Volume II)
    J-C 7, 38, 39, and 46 are for string orchestra.
    Bibliography: p.
    Contents: C major, J-C 7 (*ca.* 1730)—F major, J-C 38
(1732 or before)—G major, J-C 39 (late 1730's)—[etc.]
    1. Symphonies—Scores.   2. Symphonies (String
orchestra)—Scores.   I. Churgin, Bathia.   II. Series.
M1001.S23C52   1984   84-759414
ISBN 0-8240-3853-3

The volumes in this series have been printed on acid-free,
250-year-life paper.

Printed in the United States of America

To my sister
Professor Naomi Churgin Miller
"but, looking for a phrase,
I found none to stand beside your name"

Contents

Illustrations

Introduction

Life and works[*]

Giovanni Battista Sammartini was the seventh of eight children born to Alessio Sammartini and Gerolama Federici. The precise place and date of his birth are still unknown, though we may presume that he was born in Milan, like his sisters and brothers. The date of birth can be placed in 1700 or early in 1701, since he is said to have been seventy-four at the time of his death on 15 January 1775.[1]

Like many composers, Sammartini came from a musical family. His father was a French oboist who settled in Milan by the early 1690's, and his mother may have been a member of the Federici family of oboists active in Milan in the eighteenth

---

[*]Most of this section is drawn from the brief biography of Sammartini given in Bathia Churgin, ed., *Giovanni Battista Sammartini, Sonate a tre stromenti . . . A new edition with historical and analytical essays* (Chapel Hill: University of North Carolina Press, 1981) 3–5.

[1]Sammartini's age is stated in the main death certificate. See Newell Jenkins and Bathia Churgin, *Thematic catalogue of the works of Giovanni Battista Sammartini* (Cambridge, Mass.: Harvard University Press, 1976) 16 (abbreviated hereafter as *TCS*).

Luigi Inzaghi, "Nuova luce sulla biografia di G. B. Sammartini," *Nuova rivista musicale italiana* IX (1975) 270–71, cites two other death certificates in which Sammartini's age is given as seventy-five. For the most detailed biography of Sammartini thus far available, see *TCS*, 3–21. This biography could not take into account the new information published in Inzaghi, "Nuova luce," 267–71, which appeared too late for inclusion in the catalogue. Further biographical details have been made available in a second article by Inzaghi, "Nozze affrettate di G. B. Sammartini (da un autografo inedito)," *Nuova rivista musicale italiana* X (1976) 634–39. Among the discoveries reported there is the first known letter written in Sammartini's hand, reproduced on p. 635. The following information from Inzaghi's articles is included as a supplement and correction to the biography in *TCS*.

We now know the names, and most of the birth and death dates of the members of Sammartini's family: his father, Alessio (*ca.* 1661–5 September 1724); his mother, Gerolama Federici (*ca.* 1665–31 August 1737); and his sisters and brothers, Anna Francesca (b. 20 July 1693), Giuseppe (6 January 1695—17–23 November 1750), Maria (b. 5 February 1696), Carlo (b. 8 November 1697), the twins, Anna Maria and Rosa (19 June 1699; Rosa died 7 May 1774), and Antonio (*ca.* 1704–18 June 1743). Sammartini was married twice. His first wife was Margherita Benna (*ca.* 1692–13 November 1754), whom he married on 5 June 1727. They had one child, Marianna Rosa, born 11 September 1733 (she was a singer). Sammartini married his second wife, Rosalinda Acquania (or Acquanio), on 23 June 1755. Because of the bride's youth—she was seventeen—Sammartini requested special permission for the wedding to take place without posting banns (this is the autograph letter discovered by Inzaghi). The request was granted.

century.[2] Sammartini's older brother Giuseppe became "the greatest [oboist] that the world had ever known." He lived in London from *ca.* 1728 where he played oboe in Handel's opera orchestra and was one of the main composers of sonatas and concertos.[3] Eventually, the "London" Sammartini was distinguished from the "Milanese" Sammartini, but the compositional activity of the two brothers led to a confusion of identity in Paris, where three major collections of G. B. Sammartini (published by Leclerc as op. 2, 5, and 6) appeared under his brother's name. It is possible that another brother, Antonio, was also a composer, since some early symphonies are ascribed to him.[4]

Whether Sammartini played the oboe, like his father and brother, is unknown. Though the "Sammartini brothers" are listed as oboists in the orchestra of the Ducal theater, this indication may have referred to Antonio or Carlo Sammartini (in addition to Giuseppe) rather than Giovanni Battista, as has been thought until now.[5] Nor is there any evidence that Sammartini was a professional violinist, despite the large quantity of string music he composed. We do know, however, that Sammartini was a fine and original performer on the organ, an appropriate instrument for a composer who had a long career as a church musician.

While no information is available about Sammartini's musical education, it would seem likely that he first studied with his father and perhaps even his brother Giuseppe. Sammartini quickly gained a leading position in Milanese musical life. His name appears as a composer from the year 1724.[6] When J. J. Quantz visited Milan in 1726, he already singled out Sammartini as one of the leading church composers of the city.[7] In 1728 Sammartini was appointed organist and *maestro di cappella* of the basilica of S. Ambrogio (having held this position as a substitute from 1726), and in the same year he became *maestro di cappella* to the congregation Santissimo Entierro, which met in the Jesuit church of S. Fedele. It was for this congregation that Sammartini wrote cycles of five Lenten cantatas over the long span of years from 1725 to 1773.[8] By 1761 Sammartini was listed as *maestro di cappella* of congregations that met in eight churches, and the calendar for the year following his death gives the schedule of his activities in no fewer than eleven churches. For some years, too, Sammartini was organist in the ducal chapel S. Gottardo, finally winning the appointment as *maestro di cappella* of the Ducal court in 1768.

The Austrian administration of Lombardy from 1708 to 1796 played a significant role in reviving the cultural life of the area, especially of Milan. Sammartini's music was frequently performed in and near the city for religious and state occasions, in the colleges of noblemen, the unusual outdoor concerts near the Sforza castle, and

---

[2]Three oboists named Federici are known to have played in the opera orchestra of the Regio Ducal Teatro. They are Giuseppe, listed in 1720, and Baldassare and his son Francesco, listed for the season 1747–1748. See Mariangela Donà, "Notizie sulla famiglia Sammartini," *Nuova rivista musicale italiana* VIII (1974) 401, and *TCS*, J-C App. D-4. Composition numbers are those assigned in *TCS* (hereafter compositions will be designated by the appropriate J-C number). The symphonies are numbered according to key, not chronology. Therefore, a high number indicates a key like G or A, not a late work.

[3]The quotation comes from Sir John Hawkins, *A general history of the science and practice of music* (London: Payne, 1776; reprint, New York: Dover, 1963) II, 895. The date of Giuseppe's departure for London has been shifted from *ca.* 1727 to *ca.* 1728 because his name is included among the witnesses to the marriage of his sister Maria Maddalena on 13 February 1728 (Inzaghi, "Nuova luce," 271).

[4]See Jenkins and Churgin, *TCS*, 33, fn. 124.

[5]Jenkins and Churgin, *TCS*, 2.

[6]He composed the first aria (now lost) for the oratorio *La calunnia delusa*, a collective effort of ten Milanese composers, including Giuseppe. It was performed in Milan on 13 May 1724 (see *TCS*, App. C-18).

[7]Johann Joachim Quantz, "Lebenslauf," in Friedrich Wilhelm Marpurg, *Historisch-kritische Beyträge zur Aufnahme der Musik* (Berlin: Schützens Witwe, 1755) I, 235.

[8]Music for only eight of these cantatas has survived (J-C 117–24), together with librettos for another thirty-three cantatas and a Stabat Mater for the congregation (J-C App. C 20–34, 36–38, 40–41, 43–56).

the many private concerts in the homes of the nobility.[9] The city had a strong preference for instrumental music. It boasted many good string players and numerous composers, who provided a rich musical environment for Sammartini's creative efforts. It is no wonder that Milan was the home of the earliest symphonic school in Europe, brilliantly led by Sammartini.

Also active as a teacher, Sammartini may have taught Christoph Willibald Gluck in the period *ca. 1737–ca. 1741*. He was a frequent member of juries in the contests for posts in the churches of the city.[10] Though there is no evidence that Sammartini ever travelled beyond a sixty-mile radius of Milan, he was still able to meet some of the most important composers of the day. He knew Niccolò Jommelli, with whom he composed two cantatas in 1753 (J-C 91.1, 91.2); Luigi Boccherini, who played in orchestras under Sammartini's direction in July 1765; and Mozart, who visited Milan four times in 1770–1773. It is likely that Sammartini also came into contact with many of the German and Austrian composers who visited Milan or resided there temporarily. We now know that Johann Christian Bach, who lived in Milan from at least 1757 to 1762, was acquainted with Sammartini and that he valued his music, describing him as "a strong composer."[11] Sammartini's circle of friends included men of letters such as the poet Giuseppe Parini, and he was also a member of the celebrated Accademia dei Trasformati.[12]

The knowledge of Sammartini's music in Vienna deserves special attention. Since Milan was under Austrian domination, it was natural for Sammartini's music to have been performed in Vienna and other Austrian centers (especially monasteries) as well as Bohemia. Mention of a Sammartini Magnificat (J-C App. C-17) occurs as early as 1737–1738 in Prague. The music collection that once belonged to the famous Waldstein family (now in Prague, Národní muzeum) contains manuscript copies of thirty-three authentic symphonies by Sammartini, all but two of them middle period (see scores 4–9) and several of them in Milanese copies. This is the largest extant collection of Sammartini's symphonies, and it also holds many chamber and keyboard works.

Giuseppe Carpani, in his early biography of Haydn (published 1812), claimed that Sammartini's music was very popular in Vienna in the 1750's and that Haydn must have heard his music and have been influenced by it.[13] Much factual evidence now exists regarding the performance of Sammartini's music in Vienna, and more should be uncovered with further research. We may point to the location of the only copy of Sammartini's first opera, *Memet* (J-C 88), dated 1732, in the Abbey of Heiligenkreuz (near Vienna). It is part of a collection of primarily Viennese compositions that once belonged to Georg Reutter, Jr. (1708–1772), *Kapellmeister* of St. Stephen's Cathedral in Vienna from 1736 and the Viennese court from 1751. In Lent of 1756, a choral work (probably sacred) by Sammartini was heard in the Burgtheater,[14] and performances of a "Concert de plusieurs instruments seuls" by Sammartini occurred on 19 and 28 February 1758, again in the

---

[9]See the description of Milanese musical life in 1770 by Charles Burney, in *Dr. Burney's musical tours in Europe*, ed. Percy Scholes (London: Oxford University Press, 1959) I, 64–79.

[10]For a vivid account of the intrigue that often accompanied these competitions, see Howard Brofsky, "J. C. Bach, G. B. Sammartini, and Padre Martini: A *concorso* in Milan in 1762," *A musical offering: Essays in honor of Martin Bernstein*, ed. Edward H. Clinkscale and Claire Brook (New York: Pendragon, 1977) 63–68. This article (p. 67) contains a facsimile and English translation of Sammartini's letter to Padre Martini dated 8 September 1762.

[11]See Anne Schnoebelen, *Padre Martini's collection of letters in the Civico Museo Bibliografico Musicale in Bologna: An annotated index* (New York: Pendragon, 1979) letter no. 327, J. C. Bach to Padre Martini, 30 August 1760.

[12]Sammartini's membership in this academy is mentioned by Inzaghi, "Nuova luce," 267.

[13]See Jenkins and Churgin, *TCS*, 8.

[14]Gustav Zechmeister, *Die Wiener Theater nächts der Burg und nächts dem Kärntnerthor von 1747 bis 1776* (Vienna: H. Böhlaus Nachf., 1971) 234.

Burgtheater.[15] Most significant is a letter from Fra Giovanni Falasca to Padre G. B. Martini dated 30 June 1756, which refers to an academy on 1 July organized by Sammartini where "Sammartini wishes him to hear the compositions he intends to send to Vienna."[16] In addition, two Sammartini symphonies, the middle period J-C 4 (see Score 7) and late J-C 17, are listed in the Egk catalogue (compiled for the bishop of Olmütz) as having been obtained in Vienna before 25 November 1759. The same catalogue lists three other authentic symphonies by Sammartini in the 1760 section, symphonies probably also purchased in Vienna (these are the early J-C 33 and middle J-C 12 and 58, the last in g minor). Austrian monasteries containing copies of Sammartini's music other than Heiligenkreuz are Kremsmünster, Lambach, Melk, and Stams.

Sammartini wrote about 450 compositions in the main instrumental and vocal forms of his day. He is thus one of Italy's most versatile composers of the eighteenth century. His extant works include 67 symphonies;[17] 10 or 11 concertos; 7 orchestral concertinos; 4 marches and minuets; 6 string quintets; 27 flute and string quartets; about 177 trios, mostly for two violins and bass; over 50 flute, violin, cello, and keyboard (harpsichord and organ) sonatas; a few flute duets; 3 operas; 11 arias and vocal ensemble pieces; 8 cantatas for the Fridays in Lent; an oratorio (only one aria extant); and 16 sacred works, comprising settings of mass sections, psalm settings, litanies, the Magnificat, and Te Deum. Almost all of Sammartini's church music is lost, as are an oratorio, most of the Lenten cantatas, some secular cantatas, and several symphonies, concertos, string trios, and a concertino. To his stature as a symphonist must be added Sammartini's achievement as one of the most important Classic composers of chamber and sacred music.

[15] The information regarding the performance was discovered by Gerhard Croll and is given in Philipp Gumpenhuber, *Répertoire des toutes les spéctacles à Vienne (1758–1763)*. See Jenkins and Churgin, *TCS*, 98.

[16] The quotation is from the summary given for the letter in Schnoebelen, *Padre Martini's collection of letters*, letter no. 1956.

[17] The number of Sammartini's authentic symphonies has been reduced from 68 to 67 because it seems likely that the early symphony J-C 68 was composed by Sammartini's brother Antonio. Six late string quartets, recently discovered, have been added to this list, and the ballet J-C App. C-12 deleted, since the original attribution was not to Sammartini, as indicated by Kathleen Kuzmick Hansell, "Opera and ballet at the Regio Ducal Teatro of Milan, 1771–1776: A musical and social history" (Ph. D. diss., University of California at Berkeley, 1980) II, 958.

The symphonies: sources and chronology

A total of 135 extant symphonies are ascribed to Sammartini, of which only 67 appear to be authentic and 68 doubtful or spurious, as well as one French print. Thus, more than half the symphonies bearing Sammartini's name are probably or definitely not by the composer. Even in an age where confusions of authorship are rampant, this is a high percentage and provides further evidence of the composer's fame in his time.

Periodization of Sammartini's symphonies is largely based on stylistic characteristics established by datable works in other media (the operas of 1732, 1734, and *ca.* 1742, the Lenten cantatas of 1751, the *sonate notturne* of 1760); dated borrowings (scores 4 and 5); and dated collections, prints, and catalogue listings. Using these sources, the symphonies fall into three periods: an early period, from the late 1720's to *ca.* 1739 (18 symphonies); a middle period, from *ca.* 1740 to *ca.* 1758 (37 symphonies); and a late period, from *ca.* 1759 to *ca.* 1774 (12 symphonies). Sammartini's symphonic activity thus spans more than forty years, a fact confirmed by dated sources that exist from 1732 (see below) to 1772 (see Score 10). Few Classic symphonists besides Sammartini and Haydn composed works over such a long period of time. Sammartini's symphonies consequently have a special importance in reflecting major style trends during the formative phase of the Classic period.

Movements from two early symphonies, J-C 38/I (see Score 2) and J-C 66a/I, were incorporated in Sammartini's opera *Memet* of 1732, the opera thus providing a date for these symphonies. This is the earliest known date for Sammartini's symphonies and for the Classic symphony in general, showing that the symphony was already flourishing in the very year of Haydn's birth. Since the *Memet* symphonies exist in a fragmentary autograph that contains two other trio symphonies, one may assume that all four works were composed by 1732. To these symphonies datable in the 1730's, we may add J-C 33, whose minuet appears in a collection of Milanese minuets dated 1733–1738, and J-C 65, conducted by Vivaldi in Amsterdam on 7 January 1738.

Four early symphonies (J-C 33, 35, 37, 38) were published in Paris by Leclerc (*ca.* 1741) in a group of twelve "sonatas" Op. 2 ascribed to Giuseppe Sammartini (the print also contains four symphonies by Antonio Brioschi).[18] All these works also appear in the major source of the early symphonies—the Fonds Blancheton (Paris,

Bibliothèque nationale, Conservatoire collection). This collection of 300 orchestral and ensemble compositions (50 are missing) and 50 concertos was made for the French music patron Pierre Philibert de Blancheton (1697–1756) and has been dated *ca.* 1740–*ca.* 1744 by La Laurencie.[19] The main collection is divided into groups of 50 works given opus numbers from I to VI. Op. I and II may be dated before *ca.* 1741 since they contain works published in Sammartini's Op. 2. Unfortunately, this most important collection of early symphonies still awaits intensive research concerning its origin and chronology. After the autograph and *Memet* sources, the Fonds Blancheton provides the best available texts for Sammartini's early symphonies (see scores 1–3).

The remaining major sources of the symphonies are: the Waldstein collection in Prague, Národní muzeum, containing 33 symphonies, 11 in Milanese copies (see below); Karlsruhe, Badische Landesbibliothek, containing 13 middle symphonies, 9 in Milanese copies; Stockholm, Kungl. Musikaliska Akademiens Bibliotek, holding 17 symphonies, 14 middle period; and Paris, Bibliothèque Nationale, which, besides the 16 symphonies in the Fonds Blancheton, has the only surviving symphony autograph and modern scores (from now lost parts) of 8 late symphonies, 7 *unica*. According to the surviving sources, Sammartini's symphonies were best appreciated outside of Italy—in France, Bohemia, Germany, Sweden, and Austria.

Watermark and handwriting studies have confirmed the Milanese origin of several copies of middle-period symphonies, the most important copyists (both probably from the same copying establishment) being hands B and C,[20] which together copied fourteen middle symphonies.

---

[18]The date has been moved back from 1742 to *ca.* 1741 in Anik Devriès, *Édition et commerce de la musique gravée à Paris dans la première moitié du XVIIIe siècle: Les Boivin, Les Leclerc* (Geneva: Minkoff, 1976) 249.

[19]Lionel de La Laurencie, *Inventaire critique du Fonds Blancheton* (Paris: E. Droz, 1930) I, 13. For further remarks on the dating see my volume *The symphonies of G. B. Sammartini, Volume I: the early symphonies* (Cambridge, Mass.: Harvard University Press, 1968) 9, fn. 14.

[20]Jenkins and Churgin, *TCS*, 29–30.

Copies of twelve of these symphonies are found in Hand C, the most reliable of the symphony copyists, eleven in Prague, five in Karlsruhe, and one in Agen, France (examples of hands B and C in this volume may be found on pages xlviii, 38, 54, 96, and 142). The texts of five middle-period symphonies in this volume are based on copies in this hand, though one should remember that even such good sources lack many crucial details found only in the autograph.

Symphonic style

Sammartini's early symphonies show a hybrid Baroque-Classic style, with Classic elements predominating; the middle symphonies are fully early Classic, while the late symphonies embody many features of the later Classic idiom.

The early symphonies call for strings *a 3* or *a 4*, and all but J-C 39 (Score 3) have three movements in the plan fast-slow-fast. Most of the movements are bipartite, usually with repeat marks, and most are organized in a sonata form reflecting various stages of evolution. Many movements contain a clear structure with differentiated themes and functions, long developments, and well-defined recapitulations almost always starting with the primary theme. It is fallacious to describe these early, sometimes miniature examples of sonata form as binary or rounded binary form. Thus, the first movement of J-C 32, probably Sammartini's latest early symphony, is designated as a binary form in the third edition of Grout's *History of western music*. Binary forms, as found in some early slow movements and finales, differ markedly from sonata-form structures. Movements in simple binary form (Score 3/IV and J-C 14/II, 18/III) have little or no contrast in melody or rhythm, include little modulation, and may use parallel beginnings or endings of the two parts in the late Baroque manner. Movements in rounded binary form (more common than simple binary form—see Score 2/II and J-C 65/III) contain a key-area structure similar to sonata form.

However, they feature a carefully organized opening theme that is the only defined material in the movement and the only element fully recapitulated in the tonic (always with some variation and intensification).

The three main types of sonata form make their appearance in these symphonies: "full" sonata form, with development and recapitulation beginning with the primary theme—this type predominates; binary sonata form, with development and recapitulation of ideas after the primary theme, usually second key-area material (Score 1/I); and exposition-recap form, without a separate development section or with a very short one (J-C 15/II). While most movements are polythematic, some early examples of Classic monothematic sonata form also occur (Score 3/III, J-C 14/I). The symphonies contain brilliant examples of Classic thematic development (Score 3/I, III), and great attention is given to the integration of polythematic expositions by derivation of ideas. While some recapitulations are nearly exact, most are reformulated in various ways, sometimes radically: thematic order may be altered; themes may be omitted or changed; and new harmonic progressions and patterns of harmonic rhythm may accompany the revised thematic content. Extremely characteristic of Sammartini's early and middle symphonies is the use of thematic variants, especially of *S* and *K* ideas, in the development and recapitulation. Such variants may be altered in length, texture, melodic outline, and harmonization, and they represent a significant type of thematic development in Sammartini's music (Score 9/I/S recapitulation). These examples of reordering, rearrangement, and substitution of material are associated with the technique of the *ars combinatoria*, and they appear in Sammartini's symphonies early to late, though the most complex realizations occur in the middle period.[21]

The remarkably varied style of the early symphonies reflects the main stylistic sources of the genre (see below). The symphonies contain such characteristic Classic movement types as the 2/4 andante, 3/4 minuet, and 2/4 and 3/8 non-minuet finales. Though homophony prevails, several movements display refined textural arrangements and show new uses of counterpoint (the latter especially in J-C 14). Late Baroque influence is strongest in the slow movements, typical of the early symphonies in general (Score 1/II). It also appears in the common reliance on sequential themes for transitional, secondary, and early closing ideas, the sequential style providing sharp contrast with non-sequential opening and final themes of an exposition.

A majority of the 37 middle symphonies call for two horns or trumpets plus strings. In two cases, two oboes also play mostly *colla parte* (Score 9), and one imposing late middle work (J-C 30) contains independent oboe parts as well as horns. A group of string symphonies can still be found (Score 6), but no trio symphonies. Most symphonies conclude with 3/4 minuets, some with trios. Non-minuet finales in 3/8, C, ₵, and 12/8 occur in seven symphonies, including three of Sammartini's four middle symphonies in minor. Most of these are among Sammartini's best movements of the period (scores 5, 6, 8)—the one in

12/8 is a brilliant hunt finale. The symphonic cycles include a few two-movement symphonies (fast-minuet) and a one-movement sinfonia (J-C 27) that may be an overture to a lost vocal work.

First and third movements become longer, harmonic rhythm slower, and almost all movements are in sonata form, slow movements and minuets most often in exposition-recap form. Contrast is intensified in texture, dynamics, rhythm, and mood. Many first movements have a motoric character, using themes composed of short modules a half-measure or one-measure long. Melodic continuation by literal or varied repetition and contrast replaces the sequential expansion often found in the early style. In contrast to the early sonata-form movements, most development sections are shorter, but developmental interest is supplied by motivic development within themes, thematic derivations, thematic variants, and reformulated recapitulations that act as second developments.

In this period, Sammartini particularly exploits non-imitative counterpoint between the violins, the second violin often given an active line contrasting with the first violin, which may be exchanged in the recapitulation, especially of secondary themes. Dialogue and imitation also occur, and a new, imitative theme commonly starts the development in first movements, articulating the opening of Part II by textural contrast (scores 7–10). The independent second violin is thus a hallmark of Sammartini's style. As his style develops, texture becomes richer, incorporating more frequent imitative passages, pairing of parts, dialogues, and independent four-part string writing.

Secondary and new themes are usually presented in reduced texture, without brass and bass parts (or with punctuating bass). Several movements introduce such contrast with a new theme at the beginning of the closing section as well (J-C 49/I), the sonata-form structure with two "solo" themes becoming an important later type. Sam-

---

[21]For a discussion of the *ars combinatoria* see Leonard G. Ratner, *Classic music: Expression, form, and style* (New York: Schirmer Books, 1980) 98–102. See also my article "The recapitulation in sonata-form movements of Sammartini and early Haydn symphonies," Report of the international Haydn conference, Vienna, 1982 (forthcoming).

martini prefers a buffo to a lyrical profile theme in the secondary key, though occasional lyrical contrasts are found (Score 6/I, J-C 51/I). Many developments feature new themes and thematic variants, and these may be integrated into the recapitulation in various ways (scores 5/I, III; 7/I). Sammartini exploits new retransitional procedures including longer dominant preparations (Score 5/III) and ends several movements with short codas (scores 6/I, 8/III). The finale of J-C 46 (Score 6) presents an early example of bow sonata form, and several movements display imaginative realizations of monothematic structure or larger motivic integration (scores 5/I, III; 8/III). Three rondo minuets appear, the most extensive in J-C 52 (Score 9) containing two long trios that produce a cycle with a weighty finale. The range of expression is broadened by the often dramatic symphonies in minor. Most impressive of these is J-C 57, which anticipates later *Sturm und Drang* traits and introduces the climactic finale into the symphonic style (Score 5).

The slow movements, usually andantes and often in the tonic minor, are among Sammartini's finest creations (even Rousseau mentions them in his *Dictionnaire de musique*, article *Adagio*). Warmly lyrical, concise in form, full in texture, and richest in harmony, they contain his most personal expression, ranging from delicate charm to profound melancholy. Many are sempre piano or pianissimo (see below, p. xxiv) and most are for strings alone, though some include horns (Score 5/II) or oboes and one, in J-C 41, elaborately calls for oboes and trumpets. The minuets are greatly expanded. Many have first-movement traits in form and texture, and all are marked by an unusually wide range of rhythmic patterns and an unfailing unpredictability of phrase length. Some even contain humorous effects (J-C 48, 54).

It is in this period that the Italian overture has its strongest impact (see below, p. xxiii). One symphony, in fact (Score 4), is an early example of da capo overture form, with an interpolated slow movement.

The twelve late symphonies may have been little known in the eighteenth century since ten survive in only one source, the original parts for nine having been lost or destroyed in the Second World War. All use a basic scoring *a* 8, with independent oboes plus horns, and six contain separate cello and bass parts. Two symphonies require two violas, one has two flutes doubling the oboes in the slow movement, and one, J-C 21, contains a concerto-like movement for a solo violin. The last was perhaps intended for Felice Giardini, a famous violinist and friend of Sammartini living in London, who "approved and recommended" the print containing the symphony and two late violin concertos.

In this period, all symphonies have three movements. First and second movements increase in length. Of nine minuet finales, one includes a trio section and three are 3/8 types, not found since the early period, which feature a new *moto perpetuo* style. We find three examples of the singing allegro (as J-C 31/I) and three allegretto-like second movements called *Allegrino*, all in minor (Score 10), though the remaining slow movements are in major. One *Andante* (in J-C 2) synthesizes the learned and *galant* styles in Mozartian fashion by organizing the primary theme as a three-voice fugato, and the movement is in bow form as well.

Sonata form occurs in all movements (except in the minuet section of the minuet-trio movement). The majority of slow movements and minuets now use a full sonata form (Score 10/II), though exposition-recap form is still found in the remaining movements. Many basic traits of the sonata-form movements remain, though developments are somewhat longer, and recapitulations do not contain as many examples of thematic variants and radical reordering of material. The symphonies have longer and more varied periods, more balanced phrase structure, and a more intense lyricism that invades most of the fast movements. Fundamental changes occur in the first movements, where the motivic-figural style disappears and with it the vocabulary of pedal-point figuration, chordal patterns, and repeated-note motives. Instead there is a highly diversified melodic and rhythmic style, with many cantabile themes and motives, and often elaborate rhythms, including even thirty-second notes. A complex, nuanced harmony underlies all the movements and includes many secondary dominants, secondary triads, major-minor contrasts, dissonant chords, sequential progressions, and suspension dissonances, the last often used over pedal points to highlight important points of arrival before a new theme or in the retransition. There is even a counter-modulation in recapitulatory transitions of some movements (Score 10/II)—another forward-looking technique.

The texture resembles chamber style, with frequent dialogue among all the instruments and far greater use of canon and imitation, especially in the slow movements. Four-part string texture freely alternates with three-part, and no blanket reduction of texture occurs in any movement. All the parts participate in the presentation, continuation, or development of themes. Motion and rhythmic variety in the parts is almost constant. Few symphonies in this period exhibit such textural sophistication. An increased variety of dynamic indications supports the highly inflected style, and three short crescendos make their appearance for the first time (as in J-C 31/I/P).

Sammartini's orchestral music has a bright, transparent sound. Rhythmic effects are a prime source of vitality and structural relationship in the careful variation and contrast of rhythmic patterns and articulations, the frequent organization of rhythm in the smaller and larger dimensions by acceleration and deceleration patterns (Score 7/II), and the deft mixture of regular and irregular phrase lengths. Sammartini avoids large-scale thematic repetitions, preferring understatement to the least possibility of redundancy. The frequent elision of themes and sections produces a strong continuity that is the essence of Sammartini's style.

Stylistic sources of the early Classic symphony

The early symphony synthesized elements from the major late-Baroque orchestral and ensemble forms: the concerto, the Italian overture, the orchestral suite, and the trio sonata. So great is the variety in cycles, movement types, and scoring that this writer believes that no one genre, such as the ripieno concerto, can be singled out as the "progenitor" of the symphony, as proposed by Eugene Wolf in Series A, Volume I.

It is the trio sonata that forms the background for the trio symphony, a genre popular through the 1760's and prominent in the earliest symphonic stage. A third of Sammartini's early symphonies fall into this category (Score 2). The contributions of the trio sonata may be seen in the following aspects: the three-part texture itself, taken over into the trio symphony, usually scored for two violins and bass; the sometimes thematic second violin (see Score 1/III/recapitulation of the secondary theme) and complementary motion, voice-crossing, and linear relationships between the violins; and the soloistic character of the chamber style, reflected in richer ornamentation as well as elaboration of harmony and rhythm. The independent upper parts of the trio sonata also influenced the Baroque concerto, and it is from the concerto as well as the trio sonata itself that the independent second violin of the symphonic style originates.

The Baroque concerto, especially the examples by Vivaldi, influenced the early symphony in several ways. Certainly the ripieno or orchestral concerto provided a significant model of a self-sufficient orchestral cycle. The three-movement concerto in general was the most important model of an orchestral work that included long, well-developed slow movements and finales. Such well-balanced cycles appear in more than half the early Sammartini symphonies. Tutti-solo contrasts, associated with the solo concerto and concerto grosso, also entered the symphony as contrasts of full and reduced texture, the latter without bass or even without viola and bass (Score 1/I, II; J-C 36). In the 1740's and 1750's such contrasts became attached to specific thematic functions, reduced texture (basically piano) associated with secondary, closing, and new themes, usually in lyrical or buffo style (scores 4–10). Soloistic first violin parts in slow movements of some early symphonies (as in J-C 23, 59, and 66a—all trio symphonies) suggest the style of the solo concerto and may well have been performed by a solo violin. Ritornello form, the concerto form par excellence, can also be found in some early symphonic first movements where it is usually combined with features of sonata form.[22] However, only one movement of Sammartini's early symphonies—J-C 33/I—has this structure, and only one later movement—J-C 57/I (Score 5)—alludes to it, giving vivid proof of Sammartini's almost total rejection of this basic late Baroque structure.

Use of one key for all movements of a symphony reflects suite influence, and it occurs in many early symphonies, including three by Sammartini (as J-C 37). It was J.A.P. Schulz, in his definition of the symphony for Sulzer's *Allgemeine*

Theorie der Schönen Künste (vol. II, 1774), who first pointed to the orchestral suite (termed *partita* in the article) as the origin of the symphony. The influence of this genre can be seen most strikingly in symphonic cycles of four to six movements incorporating nondance and dance movements. Several multi-movement symphonies of this type were composed by J. J. Agrell (see Score 5 in Series C, Volume I) and other composers. One such example, original or arranged (see p. xxx), appears in Sammartini's early symphonies—J-C 39 (Score 3), which is a four-movement cycle with a giga-like third movement and minuet conclusion.

As early as 1739, the Italian overture was suggested as the model for the symphony by J. A. Scheibe,[23] and it was this view that dominated musicological thinking until recently. That the Italian overture greatly influenced the symphony cannot be denied, but as we have seen, before *ca.* 1740 it is merely one of several sources for the symphony. Only after that date does it have a strong impact.

Though the Italian overture of the 1730's is far from monolithic in style (see the varied examples in Series A, Volume I), certain standard features mark the most advanced examples by Leonardo Leo. Usually in the key of D and scored for a larger orchestra with oboes and horns, the overture differs from the three-movement concerto plan in favoring an unbalanced cycle. It thus comprises a prominent first movement, often in common time, followed by briefer second and third movements, the finale being a 3/8 minuet. Frequently, two of the movements are connected. A thin string texture predominates, the violins often playing in unison and the violas and basses in octaves. Double bars appear in the finale, if at all. The first movement has an exposition-recap form, while movements II and III are usually in binary or

---

[22]An excellent example is the Agrell symphony in E-flat, Series C, Volume I, ed. Jeannette Morgenroth Sheerin.

[23]J. A. Scheibe, *Critischer Musikus*, Neue, vermehrte und verbesserte Auflage (Leipzig: Bernhard Christophe Breitkopf, 1745) Das 65. Stück, 23 November 1739, 596.

ternary form. Uncomplicated structure and more neutral figures and figurations characterize this genre. Brilliance, brevity, simplicity—these are the principles that guide the composer, principles reflecting the function of works intended as rather unimportant preambles in the theater.

Before 1740 the influence of the overture appears mainly in the cyclical arrangement with minuet finale, found in six Sammartini symphonies, though four of the minuets are 3/4 rather than 3/8 types (Score 2). Two symphonies have rather brief second and third movements—J-C 33, 36—and connection of movements I to II occurs in J-C 33 as well. This attractive work is very much like an Italian overture in its movement types, and one wonders if it originally functioned as the overture (now missing) to Sammartini's second opera of 1734, *L'Ambizione superata dalla virtù* (J-C 89). However, the early symphonies in general, and certainly Sammartini's symphonies, differ from the overture in the scoring for strings alone, often *a 3*; in the variety of keys and meters; in the preference for a balanced cycle and fuller, more complex texture, including passages in imitative and non-imitative counterpoint; in the richer harmony; and in the typical appearance of double bars for each movement. Finally, there is a far more frequent use of sonata form, the type with long development often occurring in second and third movements as well as first movements, while exposition-recap form, if found at all, is restricted to movements II and III. Complex, imaginative structure and expressive intensity—these are the principles that guide the composer of works meant to be the focus of attention.

After 1740 the question of overture influence must be considered for each composer individually. The most important overture traits in middle and late Sammartini symphonies include: the tendency toward brief slow movements and preference for the minuet finale, though mainly the 3/4 type; use of non-repeating sonata form in several first movements; frequent head-motive beginnings and harmonic opening themes in the first movements; presentation of secondary themes in reduced texture, a type developed in overtures of the late 1730's and early 1740's; and the incorporation of wind and brass instruments. One middle symphony, J-C 44, as mentioned above, is an early example of the da capo overture form. While this list may seem formidable, Sammartini's highly sophisticated structures and textures, memorable slow movements, and dramatic symphonies in minor give his works a very different character from the Italian overtures of his contemporaries, as the symphonies in this volume will illustrate.

Performance practice[24]

In the Classic period, symphonies were performed by orchestras of various sizes from small to large. Charles Burney, who attended two private concerts (called academies) during his visit to Milan in July 1770, observed that one academy had an orchestra of 12 to 14 players that performed some symphonies by J. C. Bach, and another had 30 players, performing symphonies by J. C. Bach and Sammartini. Both groups were largely or entirely made up of amateurs.[25]

[24]For more detailed remarks about performance in the early symphonies, see my edition of the early symphonies, 11–15. For the late performance style, see my edition of Sammartini's *Sonate a tre stromenti*, 18–21.

[25]Scholes, ed., *Dr. Burney's musical tours* I, 71–72, 73–74.

We know about the composition of two festive professional orchestras led by Sammartini in July 1765 for the celebrations associated with the visit of the Infanta Maria Luisa, future wife of the Austrian archduke Leopold. The string sections comprised 15/20 violins, 3/4 violas, 4/3 cellos, and 3/4 basses. A total of 25/31 strings is certainly the maximum size for the performance of Sammartini's late symphonies (represented by Score 10), keeping in mind the softer sound of Baroque string instruments.[26] The large number of bass instruments is typical of Italian orchestras in the Classic period. An earlier festive orchestra in Amsterdam, led by Vivaldi on 7 January 1738, played an early Sammartini symphony (J-C 65) with a smaller string section of 19 players, divided 7–5–3–2–2. These string groups can serve as guides for modern performances of Sammartini's symphonies. A harpsichord continuo is required for the early and middle symphonies, but not for the late symphonies.[27]

Though the trumpet and horn parts in this volume's symphonies have the same written range, from the fourth to the twelfth harmonics (excepting the extraordinary horn parts in J-C 57, which extend over two octaves from the third to the thirteenth harmonics), the trumpets generally have a higher tessitura. Thus, the frequent horn-trumpet substitution found in some of the sources represents a practice of the period that should not be perpetuated.

[26]The orchestras performed symphonies, concertos, vocal works, and dances. They also contained a violone, probably used for the recitatives, and four oboes and four trumpets in the first orchestra, but two oboes and two trumpets in the second. It is possible that the term "trombe" referred to both trumpet and horn players (the late Sammartini symphonies call for horns, not trumpets). All four oboes and trumpets need not have played in the symphonies, since the musical program was so varied. For further information about these orchestras and Milanese orchestras in general, see especially my dissertation, "The symphonies of G. B. Sammartini" (Harvard University, 1963) I, 40–48, and Hansell, "Opera and ballet at the Regio Ducal Teatro of Milan, 1771–1776," I, 244–61.

[27]However, typical of manuscripts of the period, the early symphony autograph contains no figures. This is also true of the symphonies in this volume copied by hands B and C, except for the figured bass that appears in another hand in the Karlsruhe copy of J-C 62a (Score 8).

Most of the slow movements in this volume are marked sempre piano or have the indication piano (or pianissimo) next to the tempo; movements with no dynamic markings at all, as in scores 2 and 5, may also be of this type. The marking is most clearly defined by D. G. Türk, who states that it specifies an overall soft level but with modifications according to expressive requirements (the Affects).[28]

The wavy line found over passages in the slow movements of scores 1 and 5 is an eighteenth-century sign with several meanings. In these examples, it occurs over groups of repeated notes and signifies a slurred staccato, performed portato.[29]

In this edition all staccatos are given in stroke form, as in Sammartini's autographs. The stroke indicates a normal staccato, not a marcato, and the sharpness of the staccato should vary according to the context.

Sammartini uses a small repertoire of ornaments in the symphonies: trills, appoggiaturas, and—in the late works—a three-note turn. All the trills should start from the upper note, since the appoggiatura from above is written out in most trills found in Sammartini's opera autograph and authentic trio print. Beginning with the middle symphonies, Sammartini usually writes out the two-note suffix (Nachschlag) to the trill when he wants it (Score 8/I/3–5). The realization of appoggiaturas in the middle and late symphonies generally follows the rules given by such mid-century theorists as C.P.E. Bach, Quantz, Leopold Mozart, and Tartini, except for the appoggiatura to a dotted note, which usually takes one third rather than two thirds the value of the main note.

[28]D. G. Türk, Klavierschule (Leipzig and Halle: Published by the author, 1789; reprint, ed. Erwin R. Jacobi, Kassel: Bärenreiter, 1962) Ch. 6, par. 30, Anmerkung 1 (on the meaning of sempre piano, sempre forte). I am very grateful to my doctoral student and colleague Miriam Sheer for calling this passage to my attention.

[29]For the fullest discussion of this sign, see Dieter Lutz Trimpert, Die Quatuors concertants von Giuseppe Cambini (Tutzing: Schneider, 1967) 157–60. In the Oryx recording of Score 1/II, the conductor misinterprets this sign; his orchestra performs a trill on each repeated note under a wavy line, thus ruining the movement.

In the early symphonies the appoggiaturas are more varied in type and length; they more often include appoggiaturas from below and are sometimes more difficult to interpret. Long appoggiaturas, taking one quarter or more the value of the main note, should be performed on the beat, while short appoggiaturas should be played quickly, the accent falling on the main note. Very few ornaments appear in the late symphony, Score 10, where we find only short trills (with the suffix always written out) and one three-note turn in II/13 (called a mordent by Tartini), to be played as a turn incorporating the main note and not as a quick decoration.

In addition to the standard tempos, we find some less common indications: *Allegrissimo*, the fast extreme of *Allegro* (Score 7/I, III);[30] *Allegrino*, probably a Milanese term for *Allegretto* (Score 10/II); and *Andante moltissimo* (Score 6/II), which seems to indicate a faster rather than a slower andante tempo.[31] *Affettuoso* (Score 9/II) calls for a tempo between andante and adagio. Koch's definition of *Spiritoso* (scores 4/I, 9/III)—a favorite Sammartini marking—seems the most appropriate: "with a spirited or fiery performance."[32]

[30]Türk, *Klavierschule*, 109.

[31]Neal Zaslaw also places the related tempo *Andante molto* among the faster andante tempos in Mozart. See his article, "Mozart's tempo conventions," *Report of the eleventh congress Copenhagen 1972*, ed. Henrik Glahn and others (Copenhagen: Hansen, 1974) II, 727.

[32]H. C. Koch, *Musikalisches Lexikon* (Frankfurt: Hermann, d. J., 1802; reprint, Hildesheim: Olms, 1964) article "Con spirito, spiritoso, spirituoso."

The ten symphonies in this series

1. Symphony in C major (J-C 7)

Of the symphonies in this volume, J-C 7 is the most Baroque in style. It belongs to a group of four early symphonies whose first movements are in a type of sonata form with incomplete recapitulation (J-C 7, 15, 36) or in ritornello form (J-C 33). These works, among the earliest surviving symphonies by Sammartini, probably date from the later 1720's or early 1730's.

The long slow movement and balancing finale reflect the influence of the concerto. Use of triple meter in the first movement, though common in the early symphonies, is relatively rare later on. Tonic minor contrast in the slow movement, an early Classic preference, occurs in four early symphonies (three of them in this volume), but is most characteristic of Sammartini's middle symphonies. Typically Classic is the *Andante* tempo, together with the early Classic piano indication in the tempo heading, signifying an overall soft dynamic level with occasional intensifications when necessary.[33] The 12/8 meter suggests the siciliano, though the usual dotted rhythm is lacking. This Baroque dance type, found in only four Sammartini symphonies (three early) persists until the end of the eighteenth century. Some phrase beginnings on beat 3 indicate this is a "combined" meter of 2 × 6/8, beats 1 and 3 being equal, a metrical type often found in Sammartini's music.[34] A 2/4 *Presto* concludes the symphony. The 2/4 meter reinforces the fast tempo and is the preferred finale meter in the early symphonies though not later on. Only here do we find double bars dividing the movement into two parts organized in sonata form.

[33]For an eighteenth-century definition of this term, see p. xxiv.

[34]See the discussion of "Doppeltaktnotierung" in Helmut Hell, *Die neapolitanische Opernsinfonie in der ersten Hälfte des 18. Jahrhunderts* (Tutzing: Schneider, 1971) 75–93. See also my dissertation, I, 313–16, and the forthcoming article by Floyd K. Grave, "Common-time displacement in Mozart," *Journal of Musicology*. Several movements in this volume have this type of meter, as scores 4/I and 8/I.

On initial hearing, the first movement may sound like a late Baroque concerto movement. Outstanding Baroque traits can be found in the following elements: Sound—terraced dynamics and imitative counterpoint between the violins, the violins often crossing as well; Harmony— many sequences, including the falling-fifth type (m. 9–16), frequent seventh chords, and chromatic progressions (m. 67–70); Melody—a vocabulary of frequent leaps (like the opening theme with its broken octaves), broken chords, scale passages, repeated notes, and repeated bass figures and motives (in general, motivic and figural ideas prevail); and Rhythm—"beat" rhythm, emphasizing the single beat and its subdivision, "block" rhythms (i.e., several measures in succession in the same surface rhythm, as m. 1–4, 34–40), steady bass motion, and an overall mechanical character.

Yet, despite this seemingly overwhelming Baroque impression, significant Classic features appear in Harmony, Melody, and Growth. Long areas occur of simple tonic and dominant chords (as in m. 1–8 and 34–55). Harmonic rhythm is highly organized. In the large dimension, the exposition contains the greatest variety of harmonic rhythm, the development the fastest harmonic rhythm, and the recapitulation the slowest. Changes in harmonic rhythm articulate phrases, periods, and larger functional groupings: for example, a pedal point concludes the P section and underlines the K unit.[35] In Melody, we find pervasive two-measure groupings. In Growth, the basic descending skip motive (of various sizes from the octave to the fourth) integrates all the important material of the movement in melody and occasionally even in accompaniment (in K). While we associate monothematic structure with late Baroque form, it is not usually found in the concerto's first movement, which emphasizes contrast of ideas.

The motivic integration resembles far more Classic monothematic form, especially because it occurs within a structural framework that has much in common with binary sonata form. Key areas are clearly laid out and cadences articulate the thematic functions, which may be identified as: $1P$ (m. 1–16), $2P$ (m. 16^3–19), T (m. 20–33), S (m. 33^3–41), and K (m. 41^3–47). The contrast or development section that follows presents two new themes: $1N$ (m. 48–66^1) and $2N$ (m. 66^2–73) in e minor and a retransition (m. 74–82^2) that contrapuntally combines ideas from P, S, and $1N$ while modulating through the circle of fifths back to C. The recapitulation (m. 82^3–112) is reformulated. In binary sonata form the recapitulation usually contains only S and K material, or sometimes starts from the T function. Here, the thematic functions appear in a revised order: K^1, S^1, $2N$ (returning as a new S), K^2, codetta (P opening). Thus, K frames the recapitulation, the S and K ideas return in reversed position, one of the new development themes is integrated into the reprise, and a brief reference to

---

[35]The discussion of the symphonies in this volume draws on many terms and symbols found in Jan LaRue, *Guidelines for style analysis* (New York: Norton, 1970), especially 154–58. My explanations of the functional symbols pertain in particular to sonata and binary forms. The following symbols are used: P (themes in the primary key area); T (transition themes connecting the two main key areas); S (themes presented at or near the beginning of the second key area); SK (lyrical themes in the second key found in the closing section); K (cadential or closing themes located near the end of the secondary key area); PT (a unit that leads from P to T or S); ST (a unit that connects S themes or leads from S to K); KT (a unit that leads from K to the repetition of the exposition or into the development section); RT (my term; the retransition); and N (new material found after

the end of an exposition). Theme units are numbered as $1P$, $2P$, etc. Derivations are given in parentheses. The indications a, b, and c designate phrases, and o an introductory phrase (O, not used here, can stand for an introduction as well); x and y refer to subphrases, and m motives. The term module signifies "the pervading or characteristic growth segment" (*Guidelines*, "A cue sheet for style analysis"). Major keys are symbolized by capital letters and minor keys by lowercase letters. An indication such as V/V identifies a secondary dominant (in this case V of V). A superscript attached to a measure number indicates the beat (m. 40^2 refers to m. 40, beat 2). For the meaning of "combined" meter, see p. xxv and fn. 34. "Two-line" theme is explained on p. xli, "Exposition-recap" form is a term recently devised by Jan LaRue (see p. xviii).

P rounds off the movement. Harmonically, the recapitulation starts with unstable harmonies: *K* is presented in sequence, first on V⁷/IV–IV (touching on the first degree) and then on V⁷/V–V, the emphasis falling, however, on the main chords of the key. *S* returns over a V pedal of the home key, thus firmly establishing the key of C. Though the reformulated recapitulation may seem to be a product of an early stage of Sammartini's style, it remains a fundamental characteristic of his treatment of sonata form. While this movement shows atypical traits of sonata form as it later evolved, such as a single key for the development (if we exclude the retransition) and harmonic instability at the point of recapitulation, the basic structure of binary sonata form is clearly and imaginatively realized.

The overall style of this unusually long, serious, and eloquent *Andante* is the most Baroque of the three movements. This movement has no "standard" structure. Harmonically, Sammartini uses the key-area plan that resembles sonata form: sections in c minor and E-flat major, then a section of further modulation in A-flat, g-f-g, and a final tonic area. Each section grows progressively longer: 4½ m., 7 m., 9½ m., 12 m.[36] The plan of keys, however, does not coordinate with the thematic material. The opening phrase does not recur, and the second phrase, *2P* (starting m. 3³), returns only in the modulation section (in f). Only the *S*-like theme in E-flat (starting m. 5³) has a reprise in the tonic area, and it opens the modulation section as well, where it is extended and developed as in a development section. Slow harmonic rhythm and simple I and V harmonies also give *S* a more Classic ring. After *S* appears in the tonic area, a long, essentially new unit concludes the movement with a climactic intensity in harmony, which is the most chromatic and continuous of the movement.

The "solo"-"tutti" alternations stem from the concerto tradition. "Solo" portions here are those

without the bass part, and they occur for all of *P*, part of *S*, and the latter two thirds of the modulation section. In *S*, the entrance of the bass (with its own motive) underscores the modulation to E-flat and the return to the key of c, the final tonic section greatly strengthened by the consistent four-part texture. Imitation between the violins, found in the first movement, recurs in *2P* and the start of *S* and is another Baroque feature.

The *Presto* in sonata form[37] has so many Classic features that one hardly notices the almost steady movement of the bass in quarters, which is the only Baroque aspect. Such contrasts in style from movement to movement often appear in the earliest symphonies of Sammartini and other composers and occur in all three early symphonies in this volume. The buffo finale is a type that extends through the Classic period to Beethoven. This movement has such early buffo features as repeated notes and phrases, prominent melodic skips, syncopations, uncomplicated harmony, and surprising twists and turns. Unlike the first two movements, the texture is completely homophonic, the violins playing in unison except in the *S* theme. The static pedal harmony, delicate texture, and implied piano dynamic of *S* are traits that later become conventional in symphonic *S* themes.

The long development (26 m.) contains several characteristic procedures. Thematic recombination, a little-studied Classic technique, occurs at the opening as ideas from *P* and *S* are joined in a new phrase starting in the unexpected key of d. A long phrase sequence that follows expands the syncopated rhythmic idea into a jazzy nine-measure continuum, climaxed by a first variant of *S*. The keys rise by step, F-G-a, supporting the climactic effect in rhythm and melody, a good example of concinnity.[38]

---

[36]Elisions are not included in the measure count.

[37]Functions: *Pa*-m. 1, *b*-m. 5, *c*-m. 7; *S*-m. 10²; *K*-m. 15.

[38]This term, introduced by Jan LaRue, refers to the "highest degree of interconnection and correlation between elements." See his *Guidelines*, 16.

All the material of the miniature exposition (20 m.) is altered in the expanded recapitulation (30 m.). It is the brief, rather neutral S theme that the composer transforms into a much more defined theme, lengthened from 4 measures to 14 measures. In the tonic minor, it becomes an eight-measure period, partly repeated for an additional six measures by the second violin. The theme picks up the syncopated rhythmic figure from the development (m. 33), and it returns on the same G pedal as in the exposition, now reinterpreted as V rather than I—a typical Sammartini pun. Other functions show changes as well: Pb is now cadenced (m. 54); Pc's transitional function is made explicit by harmonic enrichment with secondary dominants and a turn to g minor; and, in place of K, a new cadential phrase derived from Pb makes a boisterous conclusion in major.

2. Symphony in F major (J-C 38)

This trio symphony is one of six composed by Sammartini solely in the early period. Such symphonies thus comprise a third of his early symphonic output.[39] The genre remained significant through the 1760's in examples by French composers and the orchestral trios by Stamitz and others.

Historically important, this symphony's first movement was used by Sammartini as the introduction to Act III of his first opera, Memet (J-C 88), the manuscript dated 1732.[40] The opera thereby dates the movement and probably the entire symphony. Movements II and III of the symphony exist in a fragmentary autograph score of four trio symphonies, all lacking first movements (J-C 23, 38, 59, 66a). The first movement of J-C 66a in the collection also appears in Memet as the introduction to Act II. It thus seems likely that all four trio symphonies in the autograph were composed by 1732, a supposition supported by the uniform handwriting and paper of the autograph as well as the stylistic homogeneity of these works. The date 1732 is the earliest known for Sammartini's symphonies and for the Classic symphony in general, though several Sammartini symphonies were probably composed before that date.

The symphony reflects the heritage of the late Baroque trio sonata in varying degrees. Least influenced is the first movement, its homophonic texture dominated by the first violin, with occasional crossing of violin II (as in S). Chamber style, however, marks the slow movement, which also includes frequent use of complementary motion between the violins, creating a dialogue effect. The minuet opens with brief imitation and provides a few measures of non-imitative counterpoint in the combination of contrasting lines (m. 18–19, 48–49).

In this work, a 2/4 Presto appears as the first rather than the more usual closing movement. A 2/4 Andante follows in the tonic minor (with a Dorian key signature), and a 3/4 Vivace minuet ends the cycle. The 2/4 slow movement became standard in the Classic style and appears in twelve of the eighteen early Sammartini symphonies, the tempo in seven of them being Andante, as in the later convention. The 3/4 minuet finale is one of five in the early symphonies, reflecting the influence of the Italian overture. Significantly, all movements of the symphony have double bars, creating two-part forms: the first and third movements are in sonata form, and the Andante is in rounded binary form.

The first movement is notable for its clear functional specialization.[41] P is the longest and

---

[39]An additional work, J-C 37, is found in both three-part and four-part versions, the filler viola part pointing to its origin as a trio symphony.

[40]For further information about the opera and problems of the dated sources, see Jenkins and Churgin, TCS.

[41]Pa-m. 1, b-m. 6, c-m. 9; PT-m. 13; T-m. 15; S-m. 21; ST-m. 27; 1K-m. 29; 2K-m. 35.

most defined theme, and its octave leaps remind us of the buffo style. Sammartini develops these leaps in the links to *T* and *K*, and includes them in *S* and *1K* as well, thus integrating the exposition with the motive. As in many early Sammartini expositions, thematic contrast is achieved by presenting *P* and *2K* as stable ideas, while *T*, *S*, and *1K* are sequential. *P* clearly states the key, ending on a V pedal; *T* provides accelerated rhythmic activity in a rising chromatic sequence; *S* features minor harmonies in a beautiful lyric, piano theme; *1K* is the active highpoint; and *2K*, picking up the syncopated figure in *P*, broadens the surface rhythm, cadencing the exposition in a repetitive pattern $(2 \times 2 + 1$ m.$)$ that remains a typical closing formula of the Classic style.

A unique feature of the movement is the composer's treatment of *S*. This remarkable theme does not start in the dominant but in the remote key of e (after *T* had led to a minor), sliding down sequentially by step to d and c. The dominant key is therefore stabilized only in the *K* area, though it had been reached earlier in *PT*. *S* recurs twice more, starting each time a tone lower, in a striking example of the *ars combinatoria* (in the development it is in d, c, and B-flat; and in the recapitulation, c and B-flat—the third key omitted for obvious tonal reasons). Functions and phrases in the exposition are also differentiated in harmonic rhythm, another Classic trait in the early symphonies. Here, the slowest harmonic rhythm occurs in functions with the richest harmony, *T* and *S*, and the fastest at the beginning and end of the exposition. *1K* is the most active unit, the fast harmonic rhythm coordinated with a shorter one-measure module and quick surface rhythm—an example of concinnity.

Another Classic aspect is the phrase structure, with its mixture of odd- and even-numbered units, the basic module being two measures. The odd subdivision of the twelve-measure *P* $(5 + 3 + 4)$ is typical of Sammartini and the period, as are the six-measure themes of *T*, *S*, and

1K.[42] The variety of phrase length and the inner structure of the themes produce an admirable rhythmic flexibility so characteristic of Sammartini throughout his life.

Sammartini organizes the development as a modified exposition, the ideas following the order of the exposition, omitting *2K*. This type of development, though infrequent in Sammartini, appears in many early Classic works, especially those by C.P.E. Bach and the young Haydn. The section ends in the relative minor, an important structural key in most Classic developments.[43]

The recurrence of themes in the development requires alteration and condensation in the recapitulation. Thus, Sammartini omits all transitional units, curtails *S*, and replaces *1K* with a new *K* idea (m. 84). This new *K* restores the tonic key in a burst of energy after *S* had turned the harmony toward the subdominant. A strengthened and extended *2K* ends the movement.

In all the early symphonies in this volume the slow movements are the most Baroque in style, a tendency in the earliest symphonies in general, but found in only five early Sammartini symphonies. Here the style is deeply expressive, featuring a rich Baroque vocabulary of seventh and ninth chords, suspensions, secondary dominants, augmented sixths, and even a poignant cross relation (m. 41).[44] The wide-ranging melodic line contains prominent diminished intervals and a wealth of melodic and rhythmic figures. The many syncopations and tied notes not only produce higher than usual rhythmic dissonance, but the entire *P* theme (m. 1–9) has an irregular

---

[42]See Judith L. Schwartz, "Thematic asymmetry in first movements of Haydn's early symphonies," *Haydn studies*, ed. Jens Peter Larsen and others (New York: Norton, 1981) 501–09.

[43]See Harold L. Andrews, "The submediant in Haydn's development sections," *Haydn studies*, 465–71.

[44]Quick simultaneous cross relations also occur between the violins in I/*T*, as in m. 17, C and C-sharp; m. 19, D and D-sharp, one example among many in the early symphonies of daring harmonic effects.

scansion,[45] all subphrases after measure 1 starting on beat 2.

Despite the Baroque language and pathos, Classic inflections appear in the clear phrase structure, varied harmonic rhythm, largely homophonic texture, and typical Classic ornaments and figures. In many ways, the movement suggests the later style of *Empfindsamkeit*, which also fuses Baroque and Classic elements.

Seven slow movements of this period are in binary rather than sonata form, five in rounded binary, as is this movement. In Sammartini's treatment of this form, clear tonal areas are projected as in sonata form, but the opening theme dominates. However, contrasting ideas may appear in the second key area and be developed in the modulation section, as we find here. This movement has four sections, which we may symbolize as *P*, *S* (m. 10), development, and *P¹*, and they expand in length, creating larger arcs of continuity: $9 + 10 || 12 + 12$ measures. Characteristically, *P* returns in a varied form, intensifying the expression toward the end of the movement. Note, too, how the lowest bass note, C, enlarges

the range of sound in the final measures.

A vigorous minuet concludes the cycle.[46] The only early 3/4 minuet in sonata form, it has an unusually balanced structure: $18 + 34$ $(16 + 18)$ measures. After a long development the recapitulation begins with *P*, but the material thereafter departs from the order of the exposition, the phrases recombining and varying motives from *P*, *T*, and *K*. Such thematic freedom after *P* in this section occurs in a few early Sammartini symphonies (as J-C 65/II) and in other works of the period.

A considerable variety of rhythmic and melodic figures and a mixture of duplets and triplets occur here as in other Sammartini minuets, as well as the inclination toward more regular four-measure phrases, so typical of the minuet style. Sammartini varies the phrase rhythm with units of six, three, and nine measures (the latter two in the development). The overlap in measure 48 between the violins produces a concluding five-measure phrase in the second violin and a strong drive to the final cadence. While the frequent repetition of the bowing pattern in measure 3 creates a Baroque effect, the variation in melodic contour is more Classical.

---

[45]Ratner, *Classic music*, 71, uses the poetic term "scansion" to denote "groups of notes, figures, measures, and phrases formed by rhythmic units."

[46]*P*-m. 1; *T*-m. 7; *K*-m. 11.

3. Symphony in G major (J-C 39)

Four movements appear in the one source for this symphony, the Fonds Blancheton, making this the only extant four-movement symphony by Sammartini. Whether the cycle is original or an arrangement by perhaps a French musician we cannot know. The cycle consists of the usual three movements, though the second movement is transitional (the only such example in Sammartini), plus a lyrical minuet with variation taken from an early trio sonata in E-flat by Sammartini. The minuet here is transposed to G and a viola part added that doubles the bass an octave higher.

What results is a kind of suite-symphony, since the last two movements are dance types—giga and minuet.[47] In a recent Oryx recording, the minuet is performed as the third movement. Not only is this order not authentic, but it destroys the surprise produced by the dramatic transition in minor leading to a light-hearted buffo movement in major, a basic constituent of the symphony's expressive plan.

---

[47]Another example of this kind of cycle is a symphony in B-flat by Fortunato Chelleri, *Six symphonies nouvelles*, No. 6 (Paris: Leclerc, *ca.* 1742–1751).

The first movement uses march rhythm, a favorite Classic topic for symphonic first movements and found in this volume in scores 4/I and 8–10/I. The third movement is a long non-minuet 3/8 finale suggesting the giga, a type often found in the early Classic symphony until the 1760's. Many fewer Baroque traits appear in this work than in scores 1 and 2. Besides the use of sequential *T* and *S* themes in the first movement, it is the transitional *Grave* that most recalls the Baroque in its tempo, dotted rhythm, chromaticism, and elaborate harmonies—note the surprising start on an E-flat chord (G: bVI)—though the augmented sixth at the half cadence is typically Classical.[48] The repeated notes seem to anticipate the repeated-note beginning of *P* in the third movement.

The first and third movements are the most advanced examples of sonata form in Sammartini's early symphonies: the first movement being polythematic and the third monothematic. The minuet is a simple binary movement, with the first violin part repeated in variation.

In the first movement, exposition, development, and recapitulation have nearly the same length: 17 measures, 16 measures, 18 measures, the long development characteristic of the early period. The almost exact recapitulation is the only such example among Sammartini's symphonic first movements, showing that he knew of this possibility but did not find it sufficiently challenging. The section, however, introduces the highest tessitura of the movement, thereby intensifying the conclusion. In the seventeen-measure exposition[49] Sammartini introduces five functions, clearly contrasted, cadenced, and integrated, as the opening two measures (*Pa*) return in a closing function in textural inversion, and *T* and *1S* share scaleline contours and syncopated melody, the latter derived from *Pb*. *P* is an advanced theme type with a chordal hammerstroke beginning, a cliché stemming from the late Baroque concerto and Italian overture that becomes almost standard in the early Classic symphony. *Pa* strongly contrasts with *Pb*, a differentiated idea that provides material for the development section. Harmonically, *T* starts in the dominant key, strengthening its cadence by V/V, a chord also found before *2S*. Both cadences are highlighted by syncopation and slower harmonic rhythm. Each function has a different pattern of harmonic rhythm. Textural differentiation also occurs within basic four-part writing, mainly by changes in the groupings of instruments and by the contrapuntal contrast (learned style) afforded by *T*.

Most impressive are the development sections in the first and third movements, the most modern and dramatic of the early symphonies. The development in movement I, divided between *P* and *T/1S*, rapidly touches on six keys after the initial recurrence of *P* on the dominant: b-D-e-a-d-g. We find such basic developmental techniques as sequence, fragmentation, inversion, textural inversion, contrapuntal intensification, reharmonization, change of mode, and thematic recombination; all are applied to the transformation of *T* and *1S* as a single idea. Modulation through the circle of fifths also becomes common in the later Classic style. The juxtaposition of major with the preceding minor at the point of recapitulation highlights the return of *P* and the tonic, making it a truly dramatic moment.

The monothematic layout of the third movement anticipates the type of structure we associate with Haydn, demonstrating the early emergence of this kind of sonata form long before Haydn made it his own. Almost all the material of this three-function exposition comes from *P*.[50] *Ta* is accompanied by the repeated notes of *Pa*; *Tb* derives from *Pa*; *S* is an exact transposition of *P* in

---

[48]A transitional slow movement of this type can be found in Vivaldi's concerto in d, Op. 3, No. 11/II.

[49]*Pa*-m. 1, *b*-m. 3; *T*-m. 5⁴; *1S*-m. 9; *2S*-m. 12; *K*-m. 16.

[50]*Pa*-m. 1; *b*-m. 5, *b*-m. 9; *Ta*-m. 13, *b*-m. 17; *S*-m. 25; *K*-m. 37.

the dominant; and the *K* figure relates to both *Pb* (downward skip) and *Ta* (downward scale). *T* offers a clear example of a modulating transition with a turn to the minor mode, both features often found in later Classic works. The fermatas add surprising halts to the rushing motion—a buffo effect.

The enormous development (50 m. to 38 m. of the exposition) brilliantly exploits intervallic expansion and variation in *Pb* and progressive fragmentation. Divided into two sections, the first starts in D, modulates to G, a, and b, and stabilizes in b. This section features expansion and inversion of *Pby* (m. 7–8), as the descending third becomes a rising sixth, and the four-measure phrases are cut to two measures (modular halving).[51] In the second section, Sammartini reverses the modulation to a and G. He first presents the skip in *Pby*, with a rising diminished fifth and new resolution, in large four-measure phrases, and then returns to *Pbx* (m. 5–6) in two-measure phrases fragmented to one measure. The modules in each sections are: 4–4–4–4–2–2–2– 2/4–4–2–2–1–1–1–1–2 (separated by an eight-measure stabilization). The harmonic rhythm reflects the modular halving, reaching its quickest

motion with the one-measure modules (two chords per measure).

As in Haydn, the monothematic structure calls for radical changes in the recapitulation, here a drastic condensation to half the length of the exposition. *P* returns complete, with a new coda-like ending drawn from the descending skip of *Pb* and an expanded *K*. In order to give sufficient weight to the tonic key, Sammartini actually returns to the tonic in the last fourteen measures of the development, preserving forward motion by the fragmentation process and sequential repetitions.

The scansion in this movement is largely symmetrical, based on units of two, four, and eight measures, while in the first movement Sammartini uses several odd-measure groups in the exposition: *P*–5 measures, *T* and *1S*–3 measures each.

In the minuet, we find a succession of phrases that are new or related by the motive found in measure 2. The usual rhyming of opening and closing phrases appears in the two main parts of the movement, but the closing rhyme of part II has a novel twist, as a variation of *T* (m. 43) surprisingly joins the end of *K*. After a long, unbroken series of four-measure phrases, the minuet closes with a group of four three-measure phrases, intensifying the drive to the final cadence.

---

[51]For the term "modular halving," see Schwartz, "Thematic asymmetry," 506.

4. *Symphony in G major (J-C 44)*

The first movement of this symphony was used by Gluck, with few changes, as the opening movement of the overture to his opera *Le nozze d'Ercole e d'Ebe*, performed in Pillnitz (near Dresden) on 29 June 1747.[52] This date establishes a *terminus ad quem* for the symphony. It was probably composed in the early or mid 1740's, possibly as the overture to Sammartini's last opera, *L'Agrippina* (J-C 90),

performed on 3 February 1743. (The overture is missing in the autograph score.)[53]

One of the earliest examples of what Jan LaRue has termed the "da capo" overture,[54] this work has a unique form in the Sammartini sym-

---

[52]For detailed information regarding Gluck's changes, see my article "Alterations in Gluck's borrowings from Sammartini," *Studi musicali* IX (1980) 117–34.

[53]The date of the opera, a correction of the date as given in Jenkins and Churgin, *TCS*, comes from Hansell, "Opera and ballet at the Regio Ducal Teatro of Milan, 1771–1776," II, 943.

[54]See his article on the sinfonia after 1700, *The new Grove dictionary*, XVII, 337, and my article "The Italian symphonic background to Haydn's early symphonies and opera overtures," *Haydn studies*, 329–36.

phonies. The da capo overture, as it evolved, was a condensation of the standard three-movement Italian overture that became popular after *ca.* 1750. The composer interpolates a slow movement at some point after the exposition in the initial allegro and then returns to a portion of the allegro movement. Thus, the three-movement cycle is reduced to two movements organized in a grand A-B-A[1] form, the finale dropping away. Here, however, Sammartini still retains the minuet conclusion. The allegro is connected to the slow movement after the recapitulation by means of a special transition that makes the change to the minor mode with a rhythmic deceleration. After the second movement ends on V, the allegro recurs in a second, abbreviated recapitulation.[55]

The trumpet parts are not perfunctory but support the rhythmic structure and sometimes offer vital rhythmic counterpoints. They even play in some piano passages, certainly unusual for the time (see III/21–22), but drop out of the slow movement, which is scored for strings alone as are most of the middle-period slow movements. In the first movement, omission of the repeat marks creates non-repeating sonata form, an influence of the Italian overture absent from the early symphonies.[56] Unlike the overture form, however, a long development appears, the connection between exposition and development being continuous. The fact that *T* and the main part of *2K* begin on beat 3 shows that the C meter is really a combined meter of $2 \times 2/4$, giving the composer an opportunity to add and delete 2/4 units and thereby increase phrase asymmetry and flexibility.[57]

The symphony's style embodies the major changes of the middle period, with most Baroque

traits eliminated. Sequential repetition, severely restricted, appears mainly in transitional or developmental passages. Literal and varied repetitions dominate many first movements (as in this example and Score 8/I), which, together with a drum bass, create a motoric style typical of the middle period. Thus, in the first movement here, the $8\frac{1}{2}$ measures of *P* are organized as: *o*-1; *a*-2×1; *b*-$3 \times \frac{1}{2} + 1\frac{1}{2}$; *b*[1]-$3 \times \frac{1}{2} + 1$. A longer sweep is given to the theme by the expanding length of the units ($1 + 2 + 3 + 2\frac{1}{2}$—the end of the theme elides with *T*), as well as a plan of accelerating harmonic rhythm in root changes found in the *a-b* phrases, which broadens at the cadence. Sammartini varies the repetitions in harmony, dynamics, or melody, and similar variations occur in most repetitive material of the movement.

Another typical feature is the chordal head motive, found exceptionally in Score 3/I of the early period. Besides asserting the key, it also underscores the start of the recapitulation. Sometimes introductory, as in this movement and in Score 9/I, it may also function as the first phrase of a dualistic theme, as in scores 3/I and 8/I.

The intricate first movement contains many contrasting ideas, carefully organized harmonically and integrated thematically. Sammartini maintains a fierce continuity by eliding all cadences between the functions and major sections. Very characteristic is the use of pedal-point harmonies on V that underlie all or most of *S* (here *1S-2S*) and on I for all or part of *K* (here *1K*). The V pedal stabilizes the harmony but still maintains the harmonic tension, which is resolved in long-range terms by the I pedal at the beginning of *K*. Thus, the latter part of the exposition makes a grand V-I progression.

Textural differentiation goes far beyond the early period. Especially important are the reduced texture given the *S* themes in the first movement, the bass omitted except for punctuation on the first beat, and the more independent second violin part in both first and second movements, where the second violin often has a fast-moving,

---

[55] A similar plan, with two recapitulations but without minuet finale, can be found even earlier in Leonardo Leo's overture to *L'Olimpiade*, 1737.

[56] *P*-m. 1; *T*-m. 9³; *1S*-m. 15; *2S*-m. 18; *3S*-m. 21; *ST*-m. 25; *1K*-m. 27; *2K*-m. 31; *KT*-m. 35.

[57] See note 34.

semi-contrapuntal line against the first violin, though coordinated with its phrase structure (I/1S, all of movement II), typical of Sammartini's middle style. Violin II also exchanges material with violin I in I/1K, and Sammartini further diversifies the texture by use of unison, two-part (unison violins, with viola and bass in octaves), and three-part string settings, sometimes changing the texture within as well as between themes. The uniform three-part string texture in the minuet, with the violins in unison, is an early feature that disappears, though the minuet usually has more unison violin passages than in other movements.

Dynamic contrasts of forte and piano, sparsely notated in the early period, appear profusely in the first movement with relation to differentiation of the S themes, contrast of repetitions (P, T, K), and close contrast of two-beat groups within the measure (3S), an accentual effect. The pianissimo specified for the second movement probably holds throughout, as in a sempre piano movement.

Several melodic figures integrate the exposition of the first movement. The third-motive in Po appears in the S themes and 2K; the repeated-note motive of Pa is picked up in ST and KT; the neighbor-note motive in Pa is embedded in 2K; the descending-scale motive in Pb can be found in the second violin counterpoint in 1S and in 3S; and the broken-chord motive in T returns in 2S and 1K. Therefore, all functions after T contain one or more derived figures.

In the development, Sammartini introduces a new counterpoint to a variant of 1S (m. 38–39), which, in altered form, becomes the top melodic line some measures later, a surprising twist (m. 45^3–47). The long development characteristically avoids a literal return of P, concentrating here on 1S and 2S. Sammartini's developments are usually organized in phrase units that present variant forms of ideas or thematic recombinations, the units moving through a series of related keys. The modulations here after D are: a, g/G, e, D, G.

Very striking is the variant form of 1S in minor (m. 36–39), varied melodically, freely inverted, and lengthened by a contrasting b phrase (m. 38–39) that introduces the new second violin counterpoint. A new unit that follows (m. 43^3) melodically links the rising third of Po with the new counterpoint of $1S^1$.

Sammartini condenses and reformulates both recapitulations. The length of recapitulation 1 is made ambiguous by another favorite device of the composer. The recapitulation proper omits both 1S and 2S, which appear in the area directly preceding the return of P: 1S as 1RT, the modulating part of the retransition in e and D, and 2S as 2RT, its dominant pedal now functioning as dominant preparation in the tonic key. Juxtaposition of S and P at the point of recapitulation contrasts the two characteristic themes of the movement. It also blurs the border between development and recapitulation, since 2S makes its tonic return in its new function as retransition, a structural pun that greatly enhances sectional continuity. After the return of P, T is omitted and 1K and 3S exchange positions. A shorter 1K recalls both the T motive and V pedal of 1–2S. It returns on the same D pedal of the exposition, now reinterpreted as G:V rather than D:I. 3S resolves the harmony with its strong cadence in G. A new 2K follows, containing a new melody over the old 2K bass line, a melody whose dotted rhythm both recalls Po and relates to P and K of the slow movement to follow. The coda-like recapitulation 2 includes only P, 3Sa, and N2K. In this movement, the thematic variants, redefinition of functions, altered thematic order, and melodic substitution provide brilliant examples of the ars combinatoria at work.

The brief slow movement is in the tonic minor and exposition-recap form. [58] It introduces a melancholy mood, with intense sighs (1S). Unified in texture and dynamics, emphasis falls on the me-

[58] P-m. 79; T-m. 85^3; 1S-m. 87; 2S-m. 91^4; K-m. 94^3; RT-m. 97^4.

lodic line, accompanied by a pizzicato bass—a new effect—and enriched by a semi-autonomous second violin part. This part, mainly in triplet motion, creates a basic meter of 12/8. The heterogeneous texture occurs in some other short slow movements and trios of minuets (see Score 9/III) and is a textural type of the period. Sammartini severely curtails the recapitulation, retaining only *P* and *K*, both of which are altered, *P* being shortened, varied melodically, and more continuous. The expressive intensity may be traced in part to the use of syncopations, suspensions, dotted (actually trochaic) rhythm, and dissonant melodic intervals.

Sammartini's middle-period minuets have a sparkle and charm lent by a much wider range of rhythmic and melodic figures than earlier, including snap rhythms and other types of syncopations. Periods composed of balanced phrases are more pronounced, as in *P* and *N* here, while Sammartini mixes phrases of even and odd lengths with considerable finesse, though this particular minuet stresses symmetry. Also in exposition-recap form,[59] the minuet contains an eight-measure bridge (*N*) after the double bar that introduces some new figures around dominant harmony. The recapitulation not only adds harmonic color (a minor) in the new transition, but this unit (m. 31–34) is surprisingly interpolated between the phrases of *P*, and K^1 presents a new concluding phrase. These alterations give the section a developmental flavor.

[59]*P*-m. 1; *T*-m. 9; *K*-m. 12^3; *N*-m. 19.

5. Symphony in G minor (J-C 57)

Sammartini wrote seven symphonies in minor, three in the early period and four in the middle period. This high proportion for a Classic composer (more than 10 percent of the extant works) is perhaps an Italian preference since it also occurs in the symphonies of Boccherini and Brunetti. Of the seven symphonies, four are in g minor (including three middle symphonies), two in c, and one in d. J-C 57 can be dated before 19 April 1749 because its finale was used by Gluck as the Introduction to Part II of his opera *La contesa dei numi*, performed on that date in Copenhagen.[60] The influence of ritornello form in the first movement suggests a date of composition early in the 1740's.

The minor mode in the Classic period, far rarer than in the Baroque, became identified with dramatic, tragic, and melancholy expression. Works in minor often inspired remarkable musical effects, and Sammartini's symphonies are no exception. While his early symphonies in minor are closer to the more impersonal Baroque usage in instrumental music, each of the middle symphonies in minor displays unusual features. The greatest of these is J-C 57, which marks the birth of the dramatic symphonic style.

In this symphony of the 1740's we find an anticipation of many characteristics of the *Sturm und Drang* style associated with Haydn's symphonies in minor of the late 1760's and early 1770's. The first and last movements contain heightened climaxes in the reformulated recapitulations, increased dissonance and chromaticism, intensified dynamic and textural contrasts (especially in the finale), and a special rhythmic tension in the first movement, which incorporates both 9/16 and 3/8 meters (though only 3/8 is specified). The horns fully participate in the dramatic style, reinforcing, doubling, and holding long, suspenseful pedals. Both outer movements are essentially monothematic, developing motives from *P*, while strong thematic contrast is provided by *N* material in the development. Few movements before Haydn's best works

[60]See my article "Alterations in Gluck's borrowings," 124–34.

display such intricate thematic and sectional relationships. The *Andante*, in simple binary form, acts as an oasis of calm amid the turmoil. Its key of E-flat (VI not III) is the key selected for the slow movement in many Classic g-minor symphonies. Though major, the key is associated with tragic and pathetic expression in the period.[61] Unlike the usual slow movement of the middle period, the horns continue playing, producing an unusually full texture. As a cycle, the symphony is also remarkable because it is one of the few Classic symphonies with a climactic finale. The 3/8 *Allegro* is 159 measures long, as opposed to 96 measures of the first movement, and it functions in every way as the culmination of the symphony, being the most complex and dramatic of the three movements.

The opening *Presto* is another example of non-repeating sonata form.[62] Sammartini unifies the movement by the dotted (actually trochaic) rhythm and repeated-note motive of *Pa*, together with the triplet rhythm and motives of *Pb*. These elements appear with variation in all later functions. An early feature is the use of the falling-fifth sequence in *Pb*, producing phrase contrast as in Score 1/I. *P* itself is heard complete three times, the theme increasing in length: 8 measures, 9 measures, 10 measures (not counting elisions). The keys for the presentations of *P* rise in thirds—g, B-flat, d. The immediate repeat of *P* in B-flat functions as *T*, another early procedure, found also in Score 1/I. Several melodic and harmonic alterations vary *T* considerably. Especially subtle is the anticipation of phrase *b* in measure 13, obscuring the cadence and promoting continuity. In *Tb* Sammartini replaces sequential by non-sequential progressions. The final and climactic appearance of *P* (P^2) occurs shortly after the beginning of the development (m. 36). In the highest register, it is a remarkable example of thematic recombination,

---

[61]See my dissertation, "The symphonies of G. B. Sammartini," I, 297–99.

[62]*P*-m. 1; *T*-m. 9; *So*-m. 18; *S*-m. 21; *K*-m. 26; *N*-m. 46.

containing references to three thematic functions—*P*, *T*, and *S*. Phrase *a* is based on *Ta*, but its fourth measure is replaced by the last measure of *So* (m. 20); *b* (m. 41–42) echoes *Tb*, but inverts the triplet motive; measures 43–45 unite *Pb*, in the triplet motion and falling-fifth harmonies, with the broader melodic outline, freely inverted, found in *S* (m. 22).

Middle-period features of the exposition include the strong cadence before *So*, the textural reduction and piano dynamic of *So*, and the stabilizing tonic pedal of *K*. As opposed to the more homophonic *P* and *T*, both *S* and *K* are contrapuntal, featuring imitative and non-imitative dialoguing violins. In *S*, variations of the two basic motives combine in a subject-countersubject arrangement presented in free voice exchange.

Each of the three thematic divisions of the movement are nearly equal in length: exposition—31 measures, development—32 measures, recapitulation—33 measures. Exposition and development elide as in Score 4/I, and a transitional phrase based on *Pa* modulates from B-flat to d for the return of *P*. A new (*N*) idea that follows introduces an unequivocal 3/8 meter, chromaticism, and biting dissonances in snap rhythm. This descending sequence (moving stepwise from d to c and B-flat) elides with the retransition (m. 58–63) based on *P*. Thus, *P* material frames the section, a development of *Pa* heard at the start and yet another variant of *Pb* heard at the end as *RTa*. The leadback in the bass actually anticipates notes 2–4 of *P* (B-flat, A, G).

Only nine measures of the exposition recur in the recapitulation, which is thoroughly reformulated. The thematic and harmonic plan may be outlined as follows: $Pa–NT(Pa)–S^1$ (around V)–N^1 (V pedal)–*S* (around I)–*NK* (*RTb*). Most dramatic is the climax area of seventeen measures emphasizing V, which contains *S* (framing *N* in a twin return on V and I) and *N*. S^1 not only stresses the highest note of the movement—d^3 (heard earlier in P^2)—but its triplet counterpoint in violin II rises rather than falls, another intensification. N^1 appears on a long, thirteen-measure V pedal. Besides reintroducing 3/8 meter, it makes a dramatic deceleration pattern of surface rhythm and harmony, coordinated with staccato-legato and forte-piano contrasts. The stretched-out V^9 chord in the last four measures is a truly Beethovenian effect. The many alterations, the recurrence of N, the intense climax—all make this recapitulation a second development section.

Only a few middle slow movements utilize a simple binary form as this *Andante*, which is dominated by its opening phrase (m. 1–4). A movement of grace and warmth, it contains a large range of rhythmic values (note the witty reversal of the dotted rhythm in m. 1^2), including genuine two-against-three rhythm. The imitative opening and further exchanges between the violins suggest trio-sonata texture, as in some slow movements of early Haydn symphonies, a Baroque influence. The more restrained expressive language is underscored by the lower tessitura of the melodic line, which never goes beyond b^{b2} in the first position of the violin.

From the abrupt chord that articulates the start of the finale, we know we are hearing an extraordinary movement.[63] The dramatic rests in the opening measure recur, either one or two beats long, as intrinsic elements of tension. The descending scale that follows the chord dominates the rich succession of ideas in the manner of a "fate" motive (here identified as *Pm*). The process resembles the technique of motivic integration found in Mozart (K. 550/I) and Beethoven (Op. 67/I). Remarkably played by two unaccompanied violins in unison, the scale descends a minor ninth and contains both E-flat and E-natural, the raised sixth degree used to avoid the augmented second. Rising and falling scale motives, on both downbeat and upbeat, can be found in the exposition in all the functions except *2K* and throughout

[63] *1P*-m. 1; *2P*-m. 9; *PT*-m. 15; *1S*-m. 27; *2S*-m. 42; *1K*-m. 52; *2K*-m. 58; *3K*-m. 62; *N*-m. 71.

the recapitulation. The clearest references to *Pm* are the shorter descending scalelines in *1S* (m. 27–29, a third), especially in the unison interruption of the theme (m. 32–33, a sixth); in the bass of *2Sa* (outlining a sixth); and in both the bass of *1K* (a fifth, in augmentation) and its melodic line (descending and rising scales of a sixth in diminution). The most important scale fragments are those spanning a third and sixth, and they are emphasized even more in the recapitulation, being twice filled in with some chromatic notes (melody, m. 131–35; bass, m. 131–40) and even lengthened to ten measures (bass, m. 131–40).

In the recapitulation, *P* does not return as we first heard it, a unique case in Sammartini's middle and late fast movements in sonata form. After a long, intense dominant preparation, the recapitulation begins in measure 114 with a piano, questioning phrase in violin I unaccompanied, the phrase derived from *2P*. This lonely voice is then answered by a full string unison forte on *Pm*, a descending sixth from B-flat twice repeated. A variation of the violin line is answered a second time by violent broken chords in the violins, followed by the original *Pm*, but now almost entirely in full string unison. This unprecedented dramatic dialogue reminds one of the solo-choral dialogue in Gluck's *Orfeo* (Act II, scene 1), where the Furies answer their terrifying "No" to Orfeo's pleas. Could Gluck have been inspired by the memory of this orchestral confrontation that he knew so well?

Again, the recapitulation is the climax area of the movement and is thoroughly transformed. After the opening dialogue, an extension of *2P* rises chromatically a fifth to high d^3 where $1K^1$ enters (in its variant form from the development), thus exchanging place with *1S*, as the bass continues its powerful descent. $1K^1$ ends on a new questioning motive of a rising scaleline of a third (m. 143), echoed an octave lower in $1S^1$ (m. 149). S^1 itself begins around the subdominant, reaching the tonic only in its fourth measure. This plagal

Score of the finale from the Symphony in G minor (J-C 57) as used by Gluck with some
alterations for the *Introduzione, Parte Seconda* in his opera *La contesa dei numi*, 1749
(*Berlin, Staatsbibliothek preussischer Kulturbesitz*)

effect intensifies the pathos and sense of despair, a pathos reinforced by the expansion of the original scaleline descent of the melody from a third to a sixth. In S^1, the questioning motive, heard twice, is twice answered by *Pm*, tutti and forte, making a final cadence with its three-note descending scale motive (m. 150, 156). This motive is reiterated a step higher in the brief reference to *3K* that ends the movement. The recapitulation is thus not only developmental—each function altered—but its new tragic expression gives it tremendous force.

A long, dramatic development (47 measures versus 66 measures of the exposition and 46 measures of the recapitulation) starts with a transposition of *Pa* in B-flat, the only "normal" gesture of the section. Sammartini then embarks on an extensive modulatory path with a new, broken-chord theme, starting on B-flat and going through the keys of E-flat, A-flat, f, b-flat. Moving down in fifths primarily, the modulations touch on such remote areas as A-flat, f, and b-flat, key relationships rarely found in developments until many years later. The unpredictable modulations with *N* are coupled with an equally unpredictable plan of piano-forte alternations that move in an acceleration-deceleration pattern, the measures grouped as follows (see m. 71–92): 4-2-2-2-2-4-6. In *N*, an agitated sixteenth-note tremolo accompaniment in violin II (derived from *2K*) and horn pedals in the background increase the high suspense of the section.

The second main part of the development (m. 93–113) is entirely forte and violent. First Sammartini presents a variant of *1K*, expanded from 6 measures to 10 measures, its first measure replaced by a rising broken-chord motive derived from *N*, its texture altered from homophonic to polyphonic by a canon between the violins, and its harmonic rhythm slowed to half the original speed. It is this intensified form of the theme that returns in the recapitulation. After passing through B-flat and E-flat, an abrupt modulation to g via a diminished seventh chord of g: V lands on

the dominant, held for eleven measures in an early example of a retransition entirely on a long V pedal. The material comes from *2K*, extended from four to eleven measures and contrapuntally enriched. An increased span and depth of sound produced by the low D in the bass, measures 105–11 (already touched on in measures 99–100), demonstrates Sammartini's special sensitivity to the placement and effect of low bass notes with relation to structure and expression. The placement here enhances the climax at the end of the development.

While this discussion has concentrated on Growth and expression, much remains to be said about other aspects that can only be suggested here. The scansion, for example, displays the usual sensitive variety of phrase lengths. It is characteristic of the composer that in the first movement the eight measures of *P* subdivide 5 + 3 and of *S* (including *So*) into 3 + 5; while the piano contrast in *K* groups the six measures as 3 + 3. More regular phrase lengths appear in the finale in comparison to those of the first movement, but even there Sammartini opposes regularity in the *P* area to irregularity in the *S* area (7 + 8, 5 + 5). In contrast, the calmer *Andante* features the most regular phrase structure: mainly two-measure modules. Even so, the last eleven measures subdivide 3 + 3 + 2 + 3, and the binary division combines not 16 + 16 but 15 + 17 measures.

No dynamic indication appears for the *Andante* in the sources, suggesting that it should be performed sempre piano. Dynamic contrasts, so prevalent in J-C 44, appear in the outer movements, most often in the finale. The *N* themes in both movements are piano, with forte contrasts or cadences. *S* areas also start piano or feature this dynamic level (as in III/*1S*). The closest dynamic contrasts occur in two-measure modules, and these appear in the finale in *PT*, *N*, and the start of the recapitulation.

While a four-part string texture marks the *Andante*, the string texture in the outer movements is basically three-part, as in J-C 44, the viola and bass doubling in octaves most of the time. Yet, considerable variety of texture comes from the various relationships between the violins, especially from imitative and non-imitative counterpoint in violin II, and the omission or punctuation of the viola/bass part. The greatest contrast in texture as well as dynamics occurs in

the finale. In addition to the usual three-part string texture we find: chordal texture, violin I alone, the two violins in unison alone, a simple and elaborated string unison, the two violins in counterpoint alone, various harmonic and contrapuntal relationships of the violins, violin I paired with the viola/bass line, and thematic viola/bass parts.

6. Symphony in G major (J-C 46)

J-C 46 is one of eight middle-period symphonies and a single movement scored for the older combination of strings *a 4*. The group includes two of the three symphonies in g minor, J-C 56 and 58. Characteristic middle-period traits are the use of common time in the first movement and the dominant major key in the second (though slow movements in the tonic minor still appear in many works, especially those in G). The 3/8 finale is one of seven non-minuet finales in the middle symphonies, four of them in 3/8. The non-minuet 3/8 type appears only in Sammartini's early symphonies and in two symphonies dated in the 1740's, J-C 10 and J-C 57, as well as J-C 46 (the 3/8 finale of J-C 58 leans toward the minuet). Use of this finale type, of occasional two-part texture with the violins in unison and the viola and bass in octaves (especially in the *Andante*, as in m. 81–85), the frequent doubling of the viola and bass, and the appearance of some long sequential ideas such as I/K and III/1N, 2N are some outstanding traits that point to a date in the 1740's for this symphony.

One is struck by the unusual length of the movements (110 m., 85 m., 152 m.), the *Andante* being the longest slow movement of the middle period and quite unlike the concise slow movement generally preferred in these years. A true chamber symphony, with few marks of the overture style, this work stresses variety of idea, texture, and structure. In I/Pb, Ta, and ST, and

III/1N there appear examples of Sammartini's favorite two-line theme type, which usually incorporates a contrasting, often faster-moving line in violin II that is contrapuntally independent though tied to the phrase structure of the first violin (here, in all but I/Pb, the moving line is exceptionally in violin I). The active accompaniments in violin II (as in I/S) represent a homophonic extreme of Sammartini's frequent contrast of the violins, which provides considerable rhythmic and linear vitality.

Textural variety here is a major component of the style. The texture ranges from two to four voices, with some themes or parts of themes in reduced texture of two voices (as II/P and III/S). Besides two-line themes, we find instances of dialoguing or alternating violins (II/S), complementary motion between the violins (II/T), the exchange of lines between the violins in later repetitions of themes (I/S, 1K), motivic viola and bass parts (II/P), pairing of the viola and bass in tenths (II/Pb) or the viola/bass line in tenths with violin II (I/3K), and divisi violas and second violins (I/T, II/P).

In the first movement[64] the many new features include the type of P theme itself. A rare example of an opening theme with lyrical as well as rhythmic qualities, P is both integrated—developing a third-motive—and balanced (3 + 4 m.)—the *b*

[64]Pa-m. 1, b-m. 4; T-m. 8; S-m. 20; ST-m. 25; 1K-m. 28; 2K-m. 34; 3K-m. 38.

phrase organized in rhythmic acceleration of both melody and harmony. *T* is non-modulating (as in J-C 57/III) and contains a series of five contrasting phrases that shift to minor at the end. The full cadence with a rest in all the parts before *S* appears in many first movements in sonata form of the period, another later Classic feature that becomes common in the 1740's. *S* here is typically on a V pedal with punctuating bass, and in a lyrical style sometimes found in middle Sammartini. Quite special is the harmonically unstable transition (*ST*) between *S* and *1K*, introducing a new kind of harmonic tension in the exposition. In this example of non-repeating sonata form, a lead connects the exposition to the long development, which emphasizes two minor keys: e (vi) and b (iii). Sammartini avoids citing *P*, characteristic of many middle-period developments, and varies material mainly from *S* and *K*. *S* both opens and closes the section, its second appearance being a tonic return as the retransition, a musical pun found in Score 4/I. Thus, in the recapitulation Sammartini moves directly from *T* into *K*, omitting *S* and *ST*.

All the movements contain codas, another new feature, and each coda expands in length. In the first movement, a coda-like insertion of two measures from *Pb* appears between *1K* and *2K*. Then a brief five-measure coda ends the movement, joining measures 1 and 7 of *P*, recalling *Ta*, and concluding with a *P* motive and a long appoggiatura—a lyrical gesture. *P* material dominates the other codas as well. The coda of $10\frac{1}{2}$ measures in the *Andante* emphasizes the chain of rising thirds in *Pb*, an essential idea of the movement. In the finale, the long coda of 29 measures brings the movement to a climax and close in a rush of motion. It reaches the highest note of the movement—e³ (heard only once before in the first movement)—and Sammartini repeats the climactic phrase an octave lower in minor, the return to the major thereafter having a triumphant ring.

The *Andante*[65] begins high on the E-string, intensifying the lyrical quality by a luminous sound. Long themes and phrases combine with an unusually complex structure in exposition-recap form. Three ideas integrate the movement: the descending broken triad in the lower voices in *P*, measures 1–2, which returns largely in the treble in *S*; the chain of rising broken-thirds in *Pb*, which recurs in *1K* and in a variant descent in *2K*, violin II; and a scalewise, directional line, rising and falling, as the long rise in *T* and the long descent in *1Kb–2K*. The recapitulation (starting in m. 38) is completely reorganized. Themes and phrases return in a new order, the juxtapositions linking units with common motives: *T–1Kb*; *S–P*; *2K–1K*.

Harmonically, the big surprise is the key of *S*, which starts in the exposition in E (A:V/V) rather than A, modulating to the expected dominant only at the end. This is one of several examples where Sammartini alters the conventional key of *S* in the exposition or recapitulation for various musical reasons, here, perhaps, to introduce greater harmonic tension in a long movement that has no separate development section.[66] After *T* returns in the tonic, *1Kb* follows still in the dominant, so that a full tonic return in the recapitulation is postponed until *S*.

The reversed order of *S* and *P* in the recapitulation echoes the same reversal found in the first movement and relates to still another example in the finale, the device linking all three movements. The brilliant, almost *moto perpetuo* finale provides another instance of non-repeating sonata form,[67] with a few long themes and two *N*-like sequences that offer contrast in the development. A bow recapitulation—surely one of the

---

[65]*Pa*-m. 1, *b*-m. 5; *T*-m. 9; *Sa*-m. 16, *b*-m. 21; *1Ka*-m. 25, *b*-m. 31; *2K*-m. 34. When themes and phrases begin on upbeats, as in *S*, the start of the unit is located in the following measure.

[66]For other examples of such tonal deviations, see Score 10/I, III and my edition of Sammartini's *Sonate a tre stromenti*, 25, 30.

[67]*P*-m. 1; *T*-m. 17; *S*-m. 31; *1N*-m. 44; *2N*-m. 62.

earliest examples of this important type of structure—begins with *T* (m. 79) and then progresses to *S* and *P*, the movement ending with the rousing coda discussed earlier. The play against symmetry permeates this movement in particular, though it can be found in all the movements. *P* itself is a long parallel period of 16 measures, but its units of 8 measures subdivide $3 + 3 + 2$. *T* is 14 measures and *S* 13 measures. Irregularities here and elsewhere stem from incomplete repetitions and sequences, added measures, and integral phrases of 3 measures, giving a superb elan to the movement. The coda itself features phrases of only 5 and 7 measures, which support the intense rhythmic drive.

One should note the sharp thematic contrast here between *P* and *S*, opposed in texture, surface rhythm (mixed eighths and sixteenths versus steady eighth-note motion), and melodic type (parallel period versus sequential expansion). A pedal point for most of *P* stabilizes the tonic at the start of the movement; the quick harmonic rhythm at the cadence is an important Classic punctuating device.[68] In contrast, *S* moves in a steady, fast harmonic rhythm. The bass part in this movement is considerably varied, the drum bass style replaced by syncopated rhythm in *T*, long tied notes in *2N*, and rushing sixteenths at the beginning of *T* and at the melodic climax in the coda.

[68]See Jan LaRue, "Harmonic rhythm in the Beethoven symphonies," *The music review* XVIII (1957) 11–12.

7. Symphony in C major (J-C 4)

This symphony is typical of many middle-period works in the scoring *a* 6 with horns, the complexity of the sonata-form first movement, the brief lyrical *Andante* for strings only and in exposition-recap form, and the fairly long 3/4 minuet finale (80 m.) also in exposition-recap form. The symphony has special interest because it was known in Vienna in the 1750's.

The less uncommon 3/4 meter of the first movement suggests the minuet topic, reinforced by the frequent repetition of the minuet rhythm ♩ ♫♫ in the horns. In the first movement we find both richness of idea and a high degree of thematic interrelationship.[69] Motives from *1P* recur in *2P*, *1S*, *2S*, and *1K*, and a motive from *2P* returns in *3K*. After the double bar, Sammartini introduces a typical imitative *N* theme in reduced texture and harmonized around G. The new theme, dynamic, and texture articulate the beginning of the development. This device often appears in Sammartini's middle and late works (see

scores 8/III, 9/I, 10/I). Though essentially new, this theme has some derived elements, as many *N* ideas in the Classic period, and provides one of several examples in this movement of thematic recombination. It incorporates the rhythmic pattern of *2P*, m. 8, the descending skips found in *2S*, and an allusion to the bass of *2K*. Again the structure includes a non-modulating *T*, a full cadence before *S*, and reduced texture in *1S* (here on a I, not V pedal). *2S* is a new theme type, with forte-piano phrase repetitions separated by an interruption with a varied reference to *1Pa*. The "solo"-"tutti" relation of *1S* to *2S* is another common feature of the period. Prominent subdominant harmony in *P*, *T*, and *S* transfers to the *K* section the task of ultimate tonal clarification, which it realizes with framing pedals on V and I.[70]

Besides the imitative *N* theme the development features contrapuntal intensification of *1Pa*,

[69]*1P*-m. 1; *2P*-m. 8; *T*-m. 12; *1S*-m. 19; *2S*-m. 24³; *1K*-m. 34; *2K*-m. 37; *3K*-m. 40; *N*-m. 45.

[70]Ratner, *Classic music*, 339, points out that in Italian music of the Classic period subdominant harmony "provided a characteristic nuance as an ornament to I, particularly at the beginning of a phrase." Many examples in Sammartini bear out this observation.

which appears in variant form with a fast-moving counterpoint in violin II (m. 48). A characteristic new type of RT (m. 61–67), in reduced texture and piano, contains a phrase sequence modulating downward by step (here d to C), each phrase starting on a V pedal that resolves at the cadence. The material used is usually S or K. Here it is a variant of $2S$, which includes a motive from $1S$ and its previous allusion to $1P$, and it eventually elides with the recapitulation. Thus, RT combines simultaneously the two main retransition procedures of the Classic period: the modulating, often sequential unit, and dominant preparation.[71] Many examples of this type of RT appear in Haydn's early symphonies, and Haydn may have been influenced in this case by the Sammartini model.[72]

In the reformulated recapitulation, only P returns unaltered. Major changes occur in T, S, and K in another striking display of the *ars combinatoria*. In place of T is a new T (NT), derived from the old T but contrapuntally and harmonically elaborated and quickened in harmonic rhythm. Sammartini then links $1S$ and $2S$ in a single period (the curtailment of $2S$ is due to its partial return in RT). $1S$ is given a small periodic form, its new answering phrase replaced in the repetition by an expressive variant of $2Sa$. Sammartini also replaces the tonic pedal of $1S$ (which would be too static here) by active chords. While S is shorter, K is enlarged and more integrative. The derivation of $1K$ from $1P$ makes possible the substitution of the more extensive $1P$ variant from the development in place of $1K$. After $2K$, Sammartini presents a new K unit based on $2Sa$, recalling RT but on a tonic pedal and cadenced by $2K$. Short appoggiaturas added to $3K$ enliven the end of the movement. The three-fold variation of

$2Sa$; the derivation of the short ornamental motive in $1P^1$ (m. 48^1) from N (m. 45^1), and its subsequent reappearance in $N1K$ and $2K$ in the recapitulation; and the reversed position of the motives in $2Sa^2$ (m. 92) and the cadence of NK (m. 107: ii-I rather than I-ii) provide additional examples of alterations in the recapitulation that affect all musical elements.

The simpler *Andante* offers relief from the intellectual play of the first movement.[73] Perfectly symmetrical (14 + 14 m., the RT of 3 m. balanced by the coda of 3 m.), the movement is a sempre piano type (here *pp*) and another case of combined meter. The emphasis falls on an expressive lyrical melody accompanied by the bass in steady quarters. Changing relationships between the violins and the varied viola part in eighths furnish some textural interest. The static melodic opening, emphatic repetitions in P and S, sigh motives in T and S, syncopated rhythm in RT, and higher range of S in the recapitulation are the main expressive details in this jewel-like movement. Typical Sammartini effects are the expanding intervals in the rising line of T (4th, 5th, 6th), which are varied and reversed in the recapitulation (7th, 6th, 5th).

An acceleration in surface rhythm takes place from P to S, moving from larger to smaller values. It is coordinated with shorter modules in T and S and faster harmonic rhythm in S (another example of concinnity). The acceleration in all elements of S intensifies greatly its expressive impact. Though RT relaxes the surface rhythm in preparation for the return of P, the coda sustains the acceleration to the movement's end. Organization of rhythm in the large dimension as illustrated here is a significant contribution by Sammartini to the Classic style.[74]

---

[71]See Beth Shamgar, "On locating the retransition in Classic sonata form," *The music review* XLII (1981) 130–43.

[72]See my article "The Italian symphonic background," 334–35, with examples from this movement and Haydn's Symphony No. 15/I.

[73]P-m. 1; T-m. 6^3; S-m. 8; RT-m. 12.

[74]In the late Notturno in C/I (*Sonate a tre stromenti*, No. 3), Sammartini organizes the development as a rhythmic deceleration, a device also found in the development of the early symphony J-C 32/I.

The minuet finale[75] characteristically exploits a wide variety of rhythmic patterns, especially snap and the usual dotted rhythms, triplets, and syncopations. A total of nineteen rhythmic patterns appear in the melodic line, and additional patterns are in the horn parts, which also contain the typical minuet rhythm found in the first movement. Here, lyrical contrast comes not with S but later, as SK in the K area where the theme has typical S-like features: a piano dynamic, differentiated four-part texture, and harmonization mostly on a V pedal. After the double bar we find a characteristic pedal point on G of six measures (with the same ambiguity of key as in the first movement). It has a bridge-like function and con-

nects back to the recapitulation. Since the pedal uses T material, Sammartini introduces a new transition in the recapitulation (m. 48) as he did in the first movement. A long nine-measure parallel period, this transition incorporates ideas from P and S; its a phrase presents complex rhythms, while a^1 is varied in melody, harmony, and texture.

As in all minuets, texture is simplified, and the violins play in unison much of the time. The composer avoids excessive symmetry, as always, and though T and S feature four-measure phrases, the other functions contain units of six measures (P, bridge), five measures (K), and three measures (end of SK). Sammartini intensifies asymmetry in the recapitulation by extending P to seven measures and ending NT with a five-measure phrase.

[75]P-m. 1; T-m. 7; S-m. 11; SK-m. 23; K-m. 30.

8. Symphony in A major (J-C 62)

This complex work is found in more eighteenth-century copies—seven—than any other middle symphony. It is the only symphony in A by Sammartini a 6, the trumpets exchanged for horns in Vienna, Paris, and Genoa. Two versions of the symphony exist: one (J-C 62a) with a well-developed finale, found in six sources; and another (J-C 62b) with a briefer, more conventional minuet finale, appearing in Genoa. The first and last movements are organized in sonata form, the first movement in the non-repeating type. An Andante e pianissimo in the tonic minor has the favored exposition-recap form found in so many slow movements of this period.

The first movement exemplifies the motoric style found in several middle symphonies (as Score 4/I).[76] A frequent drum bass in steady eighth-notes creates an intense rhythmic background for the rhythmic repetitions and contrasts, phrase asymmetries, and modular changes. Be-

cause of the combined meter, metrical displacement occurs so that some units begin on beats two or three (1K; 1Pb and 1S in the development), resulting in added half-measure units before or after the metrical shift. Extra linking measures and extensions of one or two beats complicate the metrical effect still more. Each theme has a different phrase structure, length, and rhythmic pattern. Repetitive rhythmic patterns occur in all the units. Some small melodic changes mitigate the mechanical effect of the repetitions (as in Pb), as do smaller and larger changes in the harmonic settings. The movement contains modules of $\frac{1}{2}$–$4\frac{1}{2}$ measures, the longest being 2S, which presents changing harmonies below melodic repetitions. Phrase lengths are mostly irregular. Besides three-measure phrases in 2P and 2K, extra beats or partial repetition extend the two-measure or four-measure units in 1S, 2S, and 1Ka. Only close analysis can fully reveal the artful rhythmic organization found here.[77]

[76]Pa-m. 1, b-m. 3; 2P-m. 7; Ta-m. 10, b-m. 12; 1S-m. 13⁴; 2S-m. 16; 1Ka-m. 20³, b-m. 23; 2Ka-m. 25, b-m. 28; N-m. 31.

[77]See my dissertation, "The symphonies of G. B. Sammartini," I, 309–16.

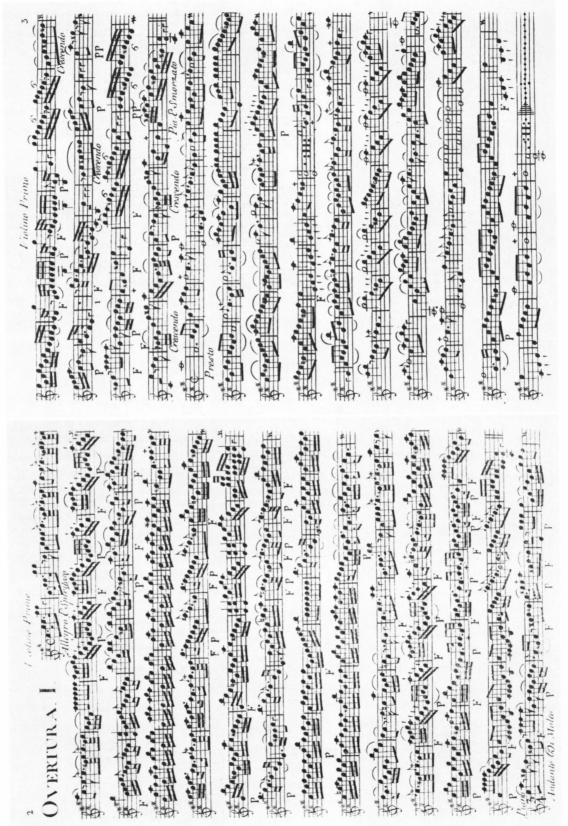

First violin part of the Venier print for the Symphony in A major (J-C 62a), showing added dynamics, ornaments, and legato bowings as well as altered tempo marks *(Paris, Bibliothèque Nationale)*

While the harmony typically emphasizes the primary chords of the key, in this movement, as in several other examples (as Score 4/I), Sammartini underlines key definition by strategic pedal points. In the exposition, pedals on V and I occur within *P* (*1Pb*, *2P*) and, more broadly, in *1S* and *2S* answered by *2K*. Pedals on V frame the development, and the recapitulation contains the same pedals as the exposition, but in mostly curtailed form. The prominent V⁷/IV in *2K* is echoed in the *K* themes of both finales, the color of flat seven in the final *K* idea being a Sammartini mannerism of the middle and late periods.

A new theme again articulates the start of a long development, this time in a homophonic setting *a 3*. Its E pedal bridges the exposition and development, the harmony becoming V⁷ of A (note the cross-relation between the violins—B-sharp/B-natural, m. 32). The *N* theme recurs in the tonic in measure 40 and is then suggested in the retransition (m. 47³–48). The A-B-A¹-C form given to the development before *RT* is one of several examples in Sammartini of a form-within-a-form structure in the development.[78] Also significant is the long *RT* based largely on V (m. 45–49). It features a variant of *1S*, the theme receiving its tonic return in this function as in scores 4/I and 6/I. The sudden shift to minor at the end offsets the major at the point of recapitulation.

Again Sammartini condenses and reformulates the recapitulation. He eliminates some repetitions, omits *T* and *1S*, and shortens *2S*, which appears in variant form with faster chord changes over its dominant pedal. Both *1K* and *2K* receive new *b* phrases, the new phrase in *2K* being a variant of *1Kb*.

Further examples appear of the active second violin in the two-line theme of *1P*, the imitation in *2Kb*, and the exchange of violin parts in the recapitulation of *2Ka*. Reduced texture highlights

1S and *N*, and the pairing of violin II and the viola in *1Pb* makes a rich sonority that points ahead to the late style.

In contrast to the limited harmonic spectrum of the *Presto*, the melancholy *Andante*[79] exploits a wide vocabulary of chromatic and dissonant chords and effects (diminished sevenths, augmented sixths, Neapolitans, secondary dominants, augmented triads, cross relations). The melodic line features typical expressive figures: sigh motives, syncopations, augmented and diminished intervals (the augmented second is especially common in Sammartini's slow movements in minor), large leaps, and repeated notes. The result is a passionate eloquence that makes this one of Sammartini's most memorable slow movements.

The second violin offers occasional rhythmic activity in *P* for bridging articulations and supporting expressive melodic gestures; one of its figures is even imitated by the first violin. Violin dialogues occur in *S* and *K*, the parts exchanged for the return of *K*. Themes are delicately interrelated: *T* begins with repeated notes recalling *P*; the sextolets in *S* return in *K* with a new dialogue-response; and the composer links the end of the exposition with the start of the recapitulation by an anticipation of *P*. A highly curtailed recapitulation omits both *T* and *S*, but the movement is expanded by an expressive coda based on *P* and heightened by Neapolitan harmony, extended syncopation, and an elaborated tonic ending.

The vivacious march-like finale[80] offers a brilliant example of motivic integration of an entire movement by a descending skip motive found in all functions and sections. In the exposition it appears at the start of *Pa* (8ve), *Pb* (11th), *T* (3rd and 4th), *S* (7th, 7th), and *Kb* (8ve, 10th, 10th). In another long development this skip motive

---

[78]For example, an exposition-recap form is found in the development of J-C 65/I.

[79]*P*-m. 1; *T*-m. 6³; *Sa*-m. 9, *b*-m. 11²; *K*-m. 16.

[80]*Pa*-m. 1, *b*-m. 5, *c*-m. 9; *T*-m. 13; *S*-m. 20; *Ka*-m. 27, *b*-m. 31.

First violin part for the second movement of the Symphony in A major (J-C 62a) in Hand C; compare the text with the version published by Venier (*Prague, Národní muzeum, Waldstein collection*)

appears in the opening unit derived from T (4th) and later as a falling and rising octave filled in triadically (m. 50–56), the descent finally expanded to a gigantic leap down of two octaves (m. 57–58). While the recapitulation omits T, a varied, more disjunct form of S includes an initial descending skip of an octave, an additional skip of the seventh, and two examples of the filled-in descending octave. Further emphasis on the octave, the interval associated with P, marks the coda (m. 91–95). Modification of the size of the skip, its rhythmic pattern, and the degree of recurrence in each unit typifies the composer's search for variety and contrast even when unifying the movement on a grand scale.

Like most Sammartini minuets, the alternate

minuet finale[81] is greatly enlivened by contrasting rhythmic patterns. Thus, for example, a new rhythmic grouping appears in measures 4–13 of the first violin part. Also characteristic of Sammartini's minuets is the textural plan of the exposition: unison violins occur in P and T, and contrasting violin parts in S and K. S features a dialogue texture and K a contrapuntal one, as violin II pairs with the viola against violin I. The play against symmetry here refreshes the brief development, with phrases of $3 + 3 + 5$ measures. Descending skips of the octave and seventh echo the march finale.

[81]P-m. 1; PT-m. 5; T-m. 8^3; S-m. 12; K-m. 15; N-m. 19.

9. Symphony in G major (J-C 52)

The scoring with oboes poses a special problem regarding modern performance of the symphony, since the oboes uniquely double violins I and II throughout the work—even in the slow movement and trios of the minuet—except for a brief solo passage at the beginning of the *Presto*'s development section. Such mechanical doubling indicates that the oboes are added parts, a Baroque practice completely at odds with the late middle style of the symphony.[82] Since *colla parte* writing produces a much larger orchestral sonority, the oboes may have been added for the Waldstein orchestra. The Vienna parts were apparently copied from this source, while the Karlsruhe and Madrid copies are *a* 6 without oboes. In performance today, the symphony could be played without oboes, the solo oboe passage arranged for strings as found in Karlsruhe (see p. 7(149)).

While the *Presto* is in sonata form and the *Affettuoso* in exposition-recap form, the minuet is

a grand five-part rondo: A-B-A¹-C-A².[83] This exceptionally long finale of 201 measures, containing a minuet in exposition-recap form and two trios as episodes, gives much weight to the end of the cycle and is without doubt Sammartini's finest minuet movement.

Several advanced features mark the first movement.[84] Perhaps the most striking is the sophisticated string texture in which the four parts are largely independent and have considerable contrast in groupings, while the bass is only occasionally in drum-bass style. Thus, P alone contains five different string groupings in nine measures, and similar variety appears in the T and K areas. Very important here are unison texture (P, end of T), dialogue and voice exchange (Ta, $1Ka$, NST—m. 80–83), the pairing of violin II and viola against violin I ($2Ka$), suspension texture (ST), and the usual imitative style of N. Besides

[82]Only one other symphony has a similar scoring, J-C 20, which probably dates from the earlier 1740's. The oboes there, however, have more independence than in J-C 52.

[83]Two other minuet rondos occur in J-C 41 and 47, both middle period.

[84]Po-m. 1, P-m. 3; T-m. 10; S-m. 17; ST-m. 26; $1K$-m. 29; $2K$-m. 36; N-m. 44.

the presence of occasional two- and three-part textures, *S* has the typical reduced texture of the period, essentially in three voices with bass and horns (in a^1) punctuating.

Sammartini projects the thematic functions with unusual clarity, and they also contain longer periods and frequent balanced phrase structure. Increased variety in surface rhythm also helps contrast the thematic material. Thus, P emphasizes unison texture; after *Po*, it makes a parallel period (4 + 3 m.), and the first phrase divides into subphrases à la Mozart. The triadic melody in march rhythm is reinforced by horns, a rare example in Sammartini of thematic brass parts. *Po* itself juxtaposes unison and reduced textures, forte and piano dynamics, march and buffo topics. The non-modulating *T* (4 + 3 m.) accelerates the surface and harmonic rhythm, ending in a unison flourish on V, a typical full cadence before *S*. Another parallel period in *S* (4 + 5 m.) establishes the second key in reduced texture and buffo style. Like *P* it contains contrasting subphrases, here motivically related: *y* develops the mordent motive of *x* in diminution, with accelerated harmonic rhythm, piano dynamic, and omitted bass. All these changes highlight the phrase division. *ST*, a directional phrase, features driving suspensions over a V pedal; and the *K* area has the quickest harmonic rhythm (2–4 chords per measure), beginning and ending on tonic pedal points.

Though Sammartini uses longer periods, he avoids exact symmetry in all units except *2K*, the functional lengths in the exposition being: 9 (2 + 7) + 7 + 9 + 3 + 7 + 8 measures. However, *Pa*, *Ta*, and *Sa* are all four-measure phrases, establishing the regularity from which the themes depart. Added symmetrical effects stem from forte-piano or piano-forte contrasts between halves of a measure (in *Pa*, *Sa*, *1Ka*, *2Ka*).

Sammartini integrates the movement in several ingenious ways. In the exposition the buffo second measure of *Po* is interpolated in *T* and at the end of *S*. The new iambic rhythm on beat 1 in the *T* version (m. 13) is then picked up in *S*. This linking technique, where a motive of a previous function appears in the following one, can also be seen in the way *Pa* uses the march rhythm in *Po*; an inversion of *Say* (m. 19–20) appears at the end of *1K* (m. 34–35), and the descending scale of that inversion continues an accelerated descent in the contrapuntal inner voices of *2Ka*; and *2Kb* includes the initial motive of *1Ka*.[85]

Tonally, the short development moves through a, G, and e, the key of e minor being most emphasized; and the section ends on a rare open cadence on e:V. Moving from this chord to G:I creates a "bifocal" cadence, a type sometimes found between large formal divisions in Classic movements.[86] The modulating sequences of the unusually long *N* theme (9 m.) are connected by an interpolated measure from *S*. This theme, like *P* and *S*, has balanced subphrases, and it combines the learned, singing, and buffo topics. In the active section that follows, Sammartini presents derived materials from *T*, *S*, *ST*, and *1K* (but not in that order), all treated differently. Most daring is the variant of *ST*, where the nearly original violin parts are reharmonized over an e:V pedal in place of D:V (m. 58–60).

Drastic cuts occur in the recapitulation of the functions that appeared in the development, including the omission of the beginning of *T*, and of *1K* as a separate function. *S* returns in complete variant form: condensed from nine to five measures, reharmonized as a descending phrase sequence based only on *Sax*, in slower harmonic rhythm, and in imitative not homophonic texture. Equally striking is the process of thematic recombination applied to the new complex setting of *ST*. This function (m. 80–85) combines the former V pedal (lengthened from three to six

[85]The first violin line in *2Ka* is also drawn from *Pb*.

[86]See the remarks on bifocal tonality in LaRue, *Guidelines*, 52–53.

measures) with free voice exchange in its first phrase that recalls the texture of *Ta*; and it adds the concluding phrase of *1K* (m. 84–85), which is drawn from the omitted *Say*. *2K* continues the process of brief citation of *1K* in other functions by replacing measures 1 and 3 of its *b* phrase by a varied reference to m. 31^3–32 of *1Kb*. These measures introduce as well a subdominant color appropriate for the close of this brilliant movement.

Like most of Sammartini's symphonic slow movements, this beautiful *Affettuoso* offers contrast in tempo, mode (tonic minor), dynamics (piano), scoring (horns omitted), character (intense lyricism), and length.[87] It also employs a simpler, mainly three-part texture (violins in unison or viola and bass in octaves). Nevertheless, Sammartini differentiates the texture according to function. The most complex setting occurs in *Tb*, where violin II has a rising line against a sigh motive in violin I, an intensification the composer uses effectively in the retransition (m. 28). Expressivity stems in part from the use of sigh motives (*P*–m. 1, *T*, *Ka*), short syncopations, ornamented first beats (*S*), and chromatic color (*Tb*, A-flat, m. 10, versus A-natural, m. 12; C-sharp in *S* and *K*; the Neapolitan in K^1 (m. 45).

In this movement, the exposition-recap form has a seven-measure bridge in which variants of *P* and *Tb* appear. Sammartini deftly varies the recapitulation, deepening the melancholy mood. Both *S* and *K* recur as variants, *S* in a small, balanced period without repetition, and *K* with new harmony and cadential endings. The V^7/IV of *T* in the exposition recurs in *S*, and the lowest bass note of the movement (D) is reserved for *Ka*. The *Ka* phrases actually appear in four versions in the movement, each presentation differing in important details. In the exposition, Sammartini also links thematically *P* and *Ta* (m. 6) and *Ta* (m. 7) with *Ka* (m. 16^2–17), and he even varies the harmony in the repeated phrases of *S*. To these

refined procedures Sammartini adds an intensive continuity produced by deceptive cadences (m. 5–6, 35–36) and elision (m. 24, 31). The musical flow enhances the expressive power of the movement.

In the five-part rondo finale the entire minuet of 54 measures acts as the refrain. For the first return of the refrain Sammartini uses only *P* of the minuet, and for the second return all of the minuet's second part. The minuet itself is in exposition-recap form,[88] with a nine-measure bridge between the sections based on *P* and *T* motives. As usual, Sammartini curtails the recapitulation, omitting *Pb* and *T*, and a cadential extension in *S*. The minuet has a three-part texture, the violins in unison except in *K*, and it is mostly forte.

The trios in e and g are extremely long (46 m., 62 m.). They omit horns and are mostly (Trio 1) or entirely (Trio 2) piano. They contrast with the minuet in their lyrical style, more refined texture, and different formal layout. These features characterize most of Sammartini's trio sections, which resemble his slow-movement style.

Trio 1 contains an open structure, without repeat marks, which could be designated as an A-B-A^1 form.[89] Its keys are e-G-e, and some opening material recurs together with a new closing idea in A^1. A retransition in unison connects the trio to the return of the refrain. Both trios begin with a descending skip, like the slow movement, and they have the same syncopated rhythm in m. 1. Both stress a half-step motive, most prominent in B of Trio 1 and the coda of Trio 2. As in the rondo minuet of J-C 47, Part II of Trio 2 opens with a triadic motive similar to the opening of Part II of the minuet. Such interrelationships between episodes and refrain are common in rondo forms of the eighteenth century.

Trio 1 exhibits the greatest textural variety in the finale, though it too has a basic three-part

---

[87]*P*-m. 1; *Ta*-m. 6, *b*-m. 8; *S*-m. 12^2; *K*-m. 16^2.

[88]*P*-m. 1; *T*-m. 10^3; *S*-m. 12; *K*-m. 18^3.

[89]A-m. 55-65; B-m. 66-81; bridge-m. 82-86; A^1-m. 87-98.

texture with viola and bass in octaves. In A, violin I dominates, while section B includes an active second violin part in a largely two-voice texture in the style of an S theme. Further variety comes from the dramatic unison at the cadence of A (m. 62–65), the unison violins ending B, the contrapuntal violin parts in the retransition to A¹, and the simple two- and one-voice violin writing in the final cadential phrases of A¹. Chromatic details, especially in the final cadence of the Trio, add to the eloquent effect of the music.

Trio 2 is one of Sammartini's most haunting creations. If Trio 1 stresses variety, Trio 2 stresses unity of material and effect. The section is in rounded binary form, the first repeat written out since the last measure has a new connection to Part II (a second ending).[90] In one texture only, Sammartini places a lyric melody in violin I, which is accompanied by a semi-contrapuntal line in nearly steady eighths in violin II and by pizzicato in the lower strings. This type of texture, with a running accompaniment in the second violin, was often used for trios and rondo episodes in symphonies of the time and even later;[91] it is also found in short slow movements (Score 4/II).

The melodic line presents subtle examples of Sammartini's technique of motivic variation, especially with respect to the dominating sigh motive of the first measure (m. 111), which is filled in, contracted in interval, inverted, and augmented. Thus, the melody seems full of variety despite the close integration. Emphasis on the sigh increases enormously the expressive impact of the music. Tension is maintained by the syncopated rhythm of the sigh and the unusual syncopated accompaniment at the melody's start, when the pizzicato punctuation enters on the weak measures 2 and 4 of the first phrase. Concern for continuity and growth may be seen in the way Sammartini treats the secondary motive of the Trio, the half-step cadential idea on the upbeat (as opposed to the downbeat sigh). This motive ends the B section (m. 147–48) and is immediately picked up for the retransition to A¹. At the end of A¹ the motive recurs on the downbeat in a new cadential phrase, integrated in this way with the sigh (m. 158–60). It then resumes its upbeat form as the dominating idea of the coda.

The phrase structure here embodies Sammartini's high art of phrase organization. Phrase lengths occur in the following succession: A: $4 + 6$ $(4 + 2)$; B: $4 + 4 + 4 + 5 + 2$; A¹: $4 + 6$ $(3 + 3)$; Coda: $7 + 1 + 5$. Extensions and asymmetries appear notably at ends of the main sections and in the coda, while most of B offers contrast in its very regularity.

[90]A–m. 111-20, repeated m. 121-31; B (based on A)–m. 132-50; A¹–m. 151-60; Coda–m. 160³-73.

[91]Examples may be found in Haydn's symphonies nos. 15 and 18; Abel's Symphony Op. 7, No. 2, Mozart's Symphony No. 14, and even in the Trio of Beethoven's Eighth Symphony, the triplet accompaniment played by a solo cello.

10. Symphony in E-flat major (J-C 26)

This late symphony embodies many new musical values. All movements are in a full sonata form, the slow movement without repeat marks.[92] The second movement is entitled *Allegrino*, a Milanese or north Italian term meaning allegretto, a favorite late Sammartini marking for the slow movement but also applied to some late first movements and minuets.[93] The *Allegrino* is in the relative minor, a choice that occurs only here and in the

[92]The thematic functions in the first movement are: *P*-m. 1; *T*-m. 8²; *1S*-m. 18; *2S*-m. 25; *K*-m. 32; *N*-m. 46. The second movement: *P*-m. 1; *T*-m. 6²; *1S*-m. 10³; *2S*-m. 14; *K*-m. 22. The third movement: *P*-m. 1; *T*-m. 7; *1S*-m. 11; *2S*-m. 15; *K*-m. 20.

[93]For further remarks about this term, see my edition of Sammartini's *Sonate a tre stromenti*, 18–19.

other late symphony in E-flat for the first time since the early period. Like other allegrinos, the movement blends playfulness and lyrical—here also melancholy—expression, the staccato and legato styles rather than the usual legato. The appearance of only one dynamic marking beyond piano—a *fp*—suggests the older sempre piano dynamic scheme. Three late symphonies contain non-minuet finales, including J-C 26. The *Allegrissimo* here is dancelike (is it a gavotte?), the fast tempo mark used, perhaps, to counter the tendency to play music of such rhythmic and textural complexity at a slower speed. Its ebullient expression is due in part to the intense rhythmic motion featuring snap rhythms and triplet sixteenths, while larger values are reserved for the surprising lyrical passages in *T* and *2S*, which produce sharp contrasts.

The scoring includes oboes and horns as the standard wind group. Oboes play in all movements, and in Classic fashion provide harmonic background, rhythmic punctuation, and melodic reinforcement, as well as some short solos (I/31, II/10, 52–54).[94] The string writing too reflects newer trends in containing fewer examples of violin doubling or octave alignment of the viola and bass. Rather, the parts are largely individualized and often treated in a chamberlike manner. The score furnishes many examples of pairing of parts, not only of the violins but of various string combinations, as well as violin canons and dialogues, and imitation between the violins or in the string group. Contrasting the same melodic line in the viola, two violins, and two oboes, as in I/29–31, and then varying the order in the recapitulation is a typical late effect. This distribution of material among all the instruments except the horns reminds us of the *quatuor concertant* style of the late eighteenth century.[95] The viola, in particular, is

emancipated far beyond contemporary practice and performs remarkable solos in the development sections of all the movements. Even the bass becomes thematic in certain passages such as I/*T*, II/*2S*. Gone is the old drum bass, replaced by a more varied and usually slower moving line, the fastest motion more often placed in the middle and upper voices while the bass supports or punctuates. The more frequent use of imitative texture reflects Sammartini's penchant for learned style in his late works, including suspension passages (as II/*2S*, III/*RT*). Fewer examples appear of non-imitative counterpoint. Thus, in the opening measures of the symphony, the second violin supplies rhythmic activity without melodic independence—this is no two-line theme as in Score 8/I.

Because of the slower bass movement and wind style, the chordal background becomes far more palpable. The harmonic spectrum in the fast movements is much wider, sharing with the slow movement the use of many secondary dominants, chromatic decorations, and appoggiatura dissonances. These appear in I/*1S* and *2S* and in III/*T* and *2S*, passages in the singing style, and these effects inflect the major with an expressive minor color. An instance of this variety of harmony is the beginning of I/*1Sa*, where the motive F-sharp-G receives three harmonizations: IV, V/ii, and ii. The richer harmony sometimes produces cross relations (II/21, 50) and dissonant melodic intervals, especially the diminished third outlined in I/*1S* and II/*2Sb* recapitulation.

Emphasis on the subdominant, found in earlier symphonies (Score 7/I), occurs in the S area of the first movement, where both *1Sa* and *2Sa* start on IV and retain A-flat (D-flat in the recapitulation) in the melody or harmony. Only the second phrase of each theme stresses V–I or V to restore the harmonic balance. Again, therefore, the final stabilizing of the key comes in the *K* area, though not without Sammartini's favorite V⁷/IV–IV progression (in both first and last movements).

With contrast and richness in so many ele-

[94]Sammartini's cantatas of the 1750's show the trend toward advanced oboe parts of this type.

[95]See Janet M. Levy, "Quatour concertant," *The new Grove dictionary*, XV, 500–01.

ments, structural complexity in this work is less evident. Still, the recapitulations in both first and second movements have some major alterations. In the allegro, *Pc* takes on a transitional function as it is newly developed with secondary dominants in the manner of a counter-modulation.[96] Sammartini then reverses the phrase order in *T* itself (probably because *Ta* was used in the retransition), *Ta* ending with the scale idea found in *1Sb* (otherwise omitted from the section). In the *Allegrino* extreme changes occur: Sammartini omits entirely the lovely nostalgic *1S* theme; between *P* and *T* he interpolates *2Sa* in a new transitional function as a counter-modulation; he recasts *2Sb*, which now contains a new climactic bar in mirror inversion (m. 50); and he ends the melancholy coda by reiterating *Pa* in a plagal setting with echoing sighs above—a most beautiful close. Even in the finale, Sammartini omits the lyrical *T*, a focus of the development, and instead gives a new

---

[96] The term "counter-modulation" refers to a modulatory digression in the recapitulation in the *P* or *T* area. See Hans David, "Mozartian modulations," *The world of Mozart*, ed. Paul Henry Lang (New York: Norton, 1963) 64–65.

T function to *1S*, which therefore retains its old dominant key for most of the theme.

A notable example of Sammartini's power of development is his transformation of the lyrical *T* in the development of the finale (m. 31–37). The latter part of the section presents a diminution of the first phrase of the idea in three melodic variants, the last being closest to the original. The theme is given new bowings (partly staccato), and treated in dialogue and then suspension texture, the latter as the main part of the retransition, in Mozartian fashion. Certain common features in all the developments help unify the symphony as a whole. These are: inclusion of *P* phrases and rhythms (unlike the middle symphonies), the prominent viola solos, and a modulation to f as one of the important keys—another example of the tendency toward the subdominant.

The first movement is the most outstanding in its intensity of contrast: of varied topics (such as the march, singing allegro, buffo, and *Sturm und Drang*), diatonic and chromatic effects, homophonic and polyphonic textures, soloistic and tutti groupings, grand and intimate expression.

General remarks on editorial method

After examining all extant sources for the symphonies in this volume, the editor has based the musical text of each work on what appears to be the best source. Some corrections, however, do stem from additional sources. Footnotes have been added on the scores that pertain to important variants, sources consulted for corrections, problematic passages, and explanations or suggestions for performance.

Original beaming and notation have been retained (except for the notation of appoggiaturas and chords), as well as the eighteenth-century

staccato mark in stroke form mentioned above (p. xxiv). All obviously wrong notes have been corrected, appoggiaturas and turn figures slurred to the main note, triplet signs added, and superfluous accidentals omitted without comment. In the first three symphonies, reproduced from another edition, editorial accidentals are indicated above the note rather than next to it in brackets, as in the remaining symphonies. Dynamic marks are abbreviated. Dashed slurs are editorial, as are dynamic marks, other performance indications, and staccatos in brackets. They have been added only when they appear in one of the instrumental parts and in parallel passages, except for some dynamic marks that are implied by notated dynamic changes, and details drawn from additional sources. In the autograph manuscripts Sammartini writes all appoggiaturas as eighth notes. In this edition, the exact length of long appoggiaturas has been indicated, short appoggiaturas shown as modern grace notes (♪). Occasionally the length of an appoggiatura is uncertain, and performers should take the solution offered as a suggestion that they may decide to interpret differently. Metronome marks have also been added to each movement as an aid for performance.[97]

[97]Many of the metronome marks follow the tempos of the symphonies as recorded or performed by Newell Jenkins.

Conclusion

The leading symphonist up to 1750, Sammartini is in many ways the father of the Classic symphony. For this writer, he is the finest symphonist before Haydn. His symphonies constitute an invaluable repertory for studying the growth of Classicism from the late 1720's to the early 1770's. Yet, Sammartini is not merely an interesting historical figure but a composer whose music is alive and appealing to modern audiences. His symphonies established a style in which fine craftsmanship; imaginative treatment of form, rhythm, and texture; integrated structure; intensive continuity; and expressive power in the slow movements are prime elements. Their importance to the development of the Classic symphony cannot be overestimated. Sammartini's symphonies share characteristics associated with both Haydn and Mozart. The formal ingenuity, reformulated recapitulations, strong continuity, and skillful phrase asymmetries resemble Haydn. The sharp contrasts, textural richness, organization of surface and harmonic rhythm, and intense lyricism remind us of Mozart. Forward-looking throughout his life, Sammartini produced early examples of techniques and styles that were explored only years later. His best symphonies have an honored place among the outstanding eighteenth-century works in the symphonic form.

Acknowledgments

This volume reflects work on the Sammartini symphonies for some twenty-five years. I am particularly grateful for the assistance throughout this long period of Dr. François Lesure of the Bibliothèque Nationale, Paris; the late Dr. Emil Hradecký and his staff of the music department of the Národní muzeum, Prague; the late Dr. Cari Johansson and Anna-Lena Holm of the Kungl. Musikaliska Akademiens Bibliotek, Stockholm; and Klaus Häfner of the Badische Landesbibliothek, Karlsruhe.

Professor Jan LaRue has not only shared with me a vast quantity of information, but also his analytical thinking about Classic music, which has deeply influenced my understanding of Sammartini's symphonies. The writings of Professor Leonard G. Ratner have been a continuous source of stimulation. I am indebted to my colleague in Sammartini research, Newell Jenkins, for the loan of microfilms and scores. His performances of Sammartini's symphonies have greatly aided my comprehension of the music, as have the performances conducted by the late G. Wallace Woodworth; Claude Monteux, who gave the first modern performance of J-C 26; and Eitan Avitsur, my colleague at Bar-Ilan University. My warm thanks also go to Hannah Abrahamson for help with photographs and proofreading; to my doctoral student, Martha Frohlich, for preparing a sim-

plified thematic catalogue of Sammartini's symphonies, which was omitted from this volume at the final stage in order to include a longer analysis section; to the Publication Committee of Bar-Ilan University for a grant toward the expense of music copying; and to Professor Barry S. Brook, Barbara B. Heyman, and Leo F. Balk of Garland Publishing for their strong support.

Finally, I wish to thank my students, past and present, for their enthusiastic response to Sammartini's symphonies, which has sustained my faith in the viability of his music.

Bathia Churgin
Kiron, Israel
July 1984

Bibliography

Barblan, Guglielmo. "Contributo alla biografia di G. B. Sanmartini alla luce dei documenti," *Festschrift für Erich Schenk*, ed. Othmar Wessely, *Studien zur Musikwissenschaft* XXV (1962) 15–27.

———. "La musica strumentale e cameristica a Milano nel'700," *Storia di Milano*. Vol. XVI. Milan: Treccani, 1963. 619–60.

———. "Sanmartini e la scuola sinfonica Milanese," *Musicisti Lombardi ed Emiliani*. Siena: Accademia musicale Chigiana, 1958. 21–40.

Bauer, Wilhelm A., and Otto Erich Deutsch, eds. *Mozart, Briefe und Aufzeichnungen*. Vol. I. Kassel: Bärenreiter, 1962.

Brofsky, Howard. "J. C. Bach, G. B. Sammartini, and Padre Martini: A *concorso* in Milan in 1762," *A musical offering: Essays in honor of Martin Bernstein*, ed. Edward A. Clinksdale and Claire Brook. New York: Pendragon, 1977. 63–68.

Burney, Charles. *A general history of music*. Vol. IV. London: Printed for the author, 1789. Modern ed. with critical and historical notes by Frank Mercer. Vol. II. New York: Dover, 1935.

———. *The present state of music in France and Italy*. London: Robson, 1771. Expanded modern ed. as *Dr. Burney's musical tours in Europe*, ed. Percy A. Scholes. Vol. I. London: Oxford University Press, 1959.

Carpani, Giuseppe. *Le Haydine*. Milan: Buccinelli, 1812.

Cesari, Gaetano. "Giorgio Giulini, musicista," *Rivista musicale italiana* XXIV (1917) 1–34, 210–71.

Churgin, Bathia. "Alterations in Gluck's borrowings from Sammartini," *Studi musicali* IX (1980) 117–34.

———. "G. B. Sammartini and the symphony," *The musical times* CXVI (1975) 26–29.

———. "The Italian symphonic background to Haydn's early symphonies and opera overtures," *Haydn studies*, ed. Jens Peter Larsen and others. New York: Norton, 1981. 329–36.

———. "New facts in Sammartini biography: The authentic print of the string trios, op. 7," *Journal of the American Musicological Society* XX (1967) 107–12.

———. "The recapitulation in sonata-form movements of Sammartini and early Haydn symphonies," Report of the international Haydn conference, Vienna, 1982 (forthcoming).

———. "The symphonies of G. B. Sammartini." 2 vols. Ph.D. diss., Harvard University, 1963.

———, ed. *Giovanni Battista Sammartini: Sonate a tre stromenti. Six notturnos for string trio, op. 7. A new edition with historical and analytical essays.* Early musical masterworks. Chapel Hill: The University of North Carolina Press, 1981.

———, ed. *The symphonies of G. B. Sammartini, Volume I: The early symphonies.* Harvard publications in music, 2. Cambridge, Mass.: Harvard University Press, 1968.

Churgin, Bathia, and Newell Jenkins. Bibliography of eighteenth-century printed collections of music by G. B. Sammartini, *Répertoire international des sources musicales (RISM)*, Series A/1: *Einzeldrucke vor 1800*, ed. Karlheinz Schlager. Kassel: Bärenreiter, 1978. VII, 324–26.

———. "Sammartini, Giovanni Battista," *Die Musik in Geschichte und Gegenwart* XI (1963) col. 1334, 1336–43; and *The new Grove dictionary* (1980) XVI, 452–57.

Devriès, Anik, and François Lesure. *Dictionnaire des éditeurs de musique française. I.: Des origines à environ 1820.* Geneva: Minkoff, 1979.

Donà, Mariangela. "Notizie sulla famiglia Sammartini," *Nuova rivista musicale italiana* VIII (1974) 400–05.

Hansell, Kathleen Kuzmick. "Opera and ballet at the Regio Ducal Teatro of Milan, 1771–1776: A musical and social history." 2 vols. Ph.D. diss., University of California at Berkeley, 1980.

Inzaghi, Luigi. "Nuova luce sulla biografia di G. B. Sammartini," *Nuova rivista musicale italiana* IX (1975) 267–71.

———. "Nozze affrettate di G. B. Sammartini," *Nuova rivista musicale italiana* X (1976) 634–39.

Jenkins, Newell. "The vocal music of G. B. Sammartini," *Chigiana* XXIV (1977) 277–309.

Johansson, Cari. *French music publishers' catalogues of the second half of the eighteenth century.* Stockholm: Publications of the Library of the Royal Swedish Academy, II, 1955.

Keller, P. Sigismund. "Mittheilungen," *Monatshefte für Musikgeschichte* VI (1874) 46–47.

La Laurencie, Lionel de. *Inventaire critique du Fonds Blancheton de la bibliothèque du Conservatoire de Paris.* Publications de la Société française de musicologie, ser. 2, vols. I and II. Paris: E. Droz, 1930–1931.

LaRue, Jan. *Guidelines for style analysis.* New York: Norton, 1970.

———. "Sinfonia after 1700," *The new Grove dictionary* (1980), XVII, 336–37; and "Symphony, I," *Ibid.*, XVIII, 438–53.

Marley, Marie Annette. "The sacred cantatas of Giovanni Battista Sammartini." Ph.D. diss., University of Cincinnati, 1978.

Mishkin, Henry. "Five autograph string quartets by Giovanni Battista Sammartini," *Journal of the American Musicological Society* VI (1953) 136–47.

Newman, William S. *The sonata in the Classic era.* 3rd ed. New York: Norton, 1983.

Paglicci-Brozzi, Antonio. *Il Regio Ducal Teatro di Milano nel secolo XVIII.* Milan: Ricordi, 1894.

Quantz, Johann Joachim. "Lebenslauf," in Friedrich Wilhelm Marpurg, *Historisch-kritische Beyträge zur Aufnahme der Musik.* Berlin: Schützens Witwe, 1755. I, 197–250.

Ratner, Leonard G. *Classic music: Expression, form, and style.* New York: Schirmer Books, 1980.

Rutová, Milada. "Valdštejnská hudební sbírka v Doksech" ["The Waldstein music archive from Doksy castle"]. 3 vols., with thematic index. Ph.D. diss., Charles University, Prague, 1971.

Saint-Foix, Georges de. "La Chronologie de l'oeuvre instrumentale de Jean Baptiste Sammartini," *Sammelbände der Internationalen Musikgesellschaft* XV (1913–1914) 308–24.

———. "Les Débuts Milanais de Gluck," *Gluck-Jahrbuch* I (1913) 28–46.

———. "Découverte de l'acte de décès de Sammartini," *Revue musicale* II (1921) 287–88.

———. "Histoire musicale: Une découverte," *Rivista musicale italiana* XXVIII (1921) 317–18.

———. "Sammartini et les chanteurs de son temps," *Rivista musicale italiana* XLIII (1939) 357–63.

Sartori, Claudio. "Giovanni Battista Sammartini e la sua corte," *Musica d'oggi* CXI (1960) 3–18.

————. "Sammartini post-mortem," *Hans Albrecht in Memoriam*, ed. Wilfried Brennecke and Hans Haase. Kassel: Bärenreiter, 1962. 153–55.

Schnoebelen, Anne. *Padre Martini's collection of letters in the Civico Museo Bibliografico Musicale in Bologna: An annotated index*. Hillsdale, N.Y.: Pendragon, 1979.

Sondheimer, Robert. "Giovanni Battista Sammartini," *Zeitschrift für Musikwissenschaft* III (1920) 83–110.

Stieger, Franz. *Opernlexikon*. Teil I: Titelkatalog. 2. Bd. Tutzing: Schneider, 1975.

Torrefranca, Fausto. "Le origini della sinfonia. Le sinfonie dell'imbrattacarte (G. B. Sanmartini)," *Rivista musicale italiana* XX (1913) 291–346; XXI (1914) 97–121, 278–312; XXII (1915) 431–46.

Weckerlin, J. B. "J. B. Sammartini et Joseph Haydn," *Le Ménestrel* LXI (1895) 3.

Zechmeister, Gustav. *Die Wiener Theater nächts der Burg und nächts dem Kärntnerthor von 1747 bis 1776*. Theatergeschichte Österreichs Band III, Heft 2. Vienna: Hermann Böhlaus Nachf., 1971.

Catalogue references for the symphonies in this volume

For further information regarding the catalogues listed below, see Barry S. Brook, Thematic catalogues in music: An annotated bibliography, New York: Pendragon, 1972. (References thereto are given in brackets.)

Breitkopf *Catalogo delle sinfonie [partite, overture, soli, duetti, trii, quatri e concerti per il violino, flauto traverso, cembalo ed altri stromenti] che si trovano in manuscritto nella officina musica di Giovanno Gottlob Immanuel Breitkopf in Lipsia Parte I–VI (1762–1765). Supplemento I-XVI (1766–1787).* [Citations in the text are from the reprint edition by Barry S. Brook (New York: Dover, 1966).] [Brook No. 167ff.]

Egk "Cathalogus über die Hochfürstlichen Musicalia und Instrumenten" (1759–1760). Státní Archiv, Olomouc (Olmütz), Czechoslovakia [Brook No. 926]

Karlsruhe Five manuscript catalogues in the Badische Landesbibliothek, Karlsruhe. The catalogues are identified by the letters A through E, and all but D are the-matic. Catalogue A is in the hand of J. M. Molter (*ca.* 1695–1765), Kapellmeister in Karlsruhe for most of the years 1722–1765. His catalogue probably dates from the period *ca.* 1755–*ca.* 1762. [Brook No. 641–44]

Lambach "Catalogus Musicalium et Instrumentorum ad Chorum Lambacensem pertinentium conscriptge MDC-CLXIIX [sic] 1768," Stiftsbibliothek, Lambach, Upper Austria. [Brook No. 708]

Sammartini Jenkins, Newell, and Bathia Churgin. *Thematic catalogue of the works of Giovanni Battista Sammartini: Orchestral and vocal music*. Cambridge, Mass.: Harvard University Press, 1976. Published for the American Musicological Society [Brook No. 1136]

The Symphony 1720–1840
Barry S. Brook, Editor-in-Chief   Series A-Volume II-Score 1

Symphony in C major

Them. Index J-C 7

Giovanni Battista Sammartini

Milan? 1700 or 1701–1775 Milan

Edited by Bathia Churgin

p. 3 (3)

p. 9 (9)

p. 11 (11)

Instrumentation: 2 violins, viola, bass

Date: Before *ca.* 1741 (date of the Fonds Blancheton Op. II). On the basis of style, *ca.* 1730.

Source used for this edition: Manuscript parts in Paris, Bibliothèque Nationale, Conservatoire collection, Fonds Blancheton Rés. F. 442, Op. II/87, "Sonata Del Sigr. Gio Baptista St. Martino a 4° Stromenti" (source A).

Other sources: (In parts unless otherwise indicated) (1) Lund (Sweden), Universitetsbiblioteket, Wenster Litt. C 4, Sinfonia, San Martini (source B); and another copy, Wenster Litt. L 50, Sonata, anonymous (without viola; the poorest version); (2) Dresden, Sächsische Landesbibliothek Mus. 2/N/24,5, Sinfonia, anonymous (score; movement III missing).

Modern edition: Bathia Churgin, ed., *The symphonies of G. B. Sammartini. Volume I: The early symphonies.* Harvard publications in music, 2. (Cambridge, Mass.: Harvard University Press, 1968). Sym. No. 1.

Recording: Newell Jenkins, conductor, Angelicum Orchestra of Milan, Nonesuch H-1162 (mono) or H-71162 (stereo)

Editorial remarks: The first Lund copy and the Dresden score contain a different and inferior viola part.

Garland Publishing, Inc.   New York & London   1984

First violin part of the first and second movements for the Symphony in C major (J-C 7) (Paris, Bibliothèque Nationale, Conservatoire collection, Fonds Blancheton)

Symphony in C major

Them. Index J-C 7

Edited by Bathia Churgin

I

* m. 19, *d* in both sources.

* m. 41: The chord as given follows the parallel passage in m. 98.

source A   source B

* m. 66: Bowing here and in parallel measures from source B.

II

* m. 32: *f* in source A, *c* in source B.

III

Presto (♩ = *ca.* 132)

* m. 20: The fermata applies only to the repeat of the section.

The Symphony 1720–1840
Barry S. Brook, Editor-in-Chief   Series A-Volume II-Score 2

Symphony in F major
Them. Index J-C 38

Giovanni Battista Sammartini
Milan? 1700 or 1701–1775 Milan

Edited by Bathia Churgin

Instrumentation: 2 violins, bass

Date: 1732 or before (date of Sammartini's opera *Memet*)

Sources used for this edition: For movements II and III the fragmentary autograph score (title page and first movements lacking) of four early trio symphonies, Paris, Bibliothèque Nationale Rés. Vma. ms. 988, ff. 1–3r (source A). For the first movement, the score of the "Introdutione" to Act III of Sammartini's first opera, "Memet Tragedia. Musica Del Sigr. Gio. Batta: St. Martino, 1732," Stift Heiligenkreuz, Lower Austria, B IV (source A¹).

Other sources: (In parts) (1) Paris, Bibliothèque Nationale, Conservatoire collection, Fonds Blancheton Rés. F. 441, Op. I/17, Sinfonia, Martini (source B); (2) printed parts, Paris, Leclerc, *ca.* 1741, *XII Sonate*, Op. II/1 (erroneously ascribed to Giuseppe Sammartini), copy Paris, Bibliothèque Nationale, Conservatoire collection K. 5511; (3) Paris, Bibliothèque Nationale, Conservatoire collection D.11.180, Sonata a Tré (Overtura on the inside pages), Martino (based on the Leclerc edition).

Modern edition: Bathia Churgin, ed. *The symphonies of G. B. Sammartini. Volume I: The early symphonies.* Harvard publications in music, 2. Cambridge, Mass.: Harvard University Press, 1968. Sym. No. 12.

Editorial remarks: The score of *Memet*, J-C 88, was discovered by Jan LaRue in 1955. The manuscript is north Italian in origin and contains the first movements of two early Sammartini symphonies used as introductions to Act II (J-C 66a) and Act III (J-C 38) of the opera, thereby dating the symphonies. These are the earliest dated symphonies by Sammartini. An added viola part, probably written by Sammartini, appears in the overture version of J-C 38/I. Because of its interest as a model of such added filler parts in the period, and because of its possible authenticity, it has been included in this edition in small notes. A performance of the opera in Vienna is suggested by the fact that the score belongs to a collection of primarily Viennese works once owned by the Viennese composer Georg von Reutter, Jr. (1708–1772).

Folio 2v of the autograph score for the third movement of the Symphony in F major (J-C 38)
(*Paris, Bibliothèque Nationale*)

Garland Publishing, Inc. New York & London 1984

Symphony in F major

Them. Index J-C 38

Edited by Bathia Churgin

Giovanni Battista Sammartini

I

* m. 21: In source A′, the bowings in mm. 21-26 and parallel passages are so inconsistent that the bowings from source B have been used instead.

** m. 21: In vn. I, *pp* in sources A′ and B, and in B for all further appearances of the theme.

* m. 59: The *forte* in vn. I, source A' appears over the 2nd eighth.

II

Andante ($\flat$ = *ca.* 72)

Violino I

Violino II

Basso

* m. 20: The trill in the autograph appears on the $b\flat$ in vn. II.

III

The Symphony 1720–1840
Barry S. Brook, Editor-in-Chief   Series A-Volume II-Score 3

Symphony in G major
Them. Index J-C 39

Giovanni Battista Sammartini
Milan? 1700 or 1701–1775 Milan

Edited by Bathia Churgin

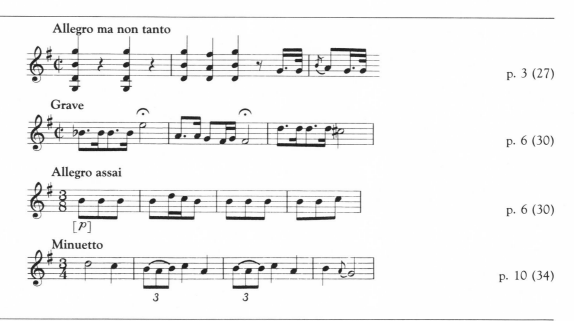

Allegro ma non tanto — p. 3 (27)

Grave — p. 6 (30)

Allegro assai — p. 6 (30)

Minuetto — p. 10 (34)

Instrumentation: 2 violins, viola, bass

Date: Before *ca.* 1744 (date of the Fonds Blancheton Op. III). On the basis of style, in the later 1730's.

Source used for this edition: Manuscript parts in Paris, Bibliothèque Nationale, Conservatoire collection, Fonds Blancheton Rés. F. 443, Op. III/150, "Sinfonia Del Sigr. Gio. Bap. St. Martini a 4º. Stromenti."

Other sources: Of the minuet only (in parts). (1) Final movement of a trio sonata in E-flat major: Fonds Blancheton Op. III/121; (2) printed parts, London, Simpson, 1744, *Six sonatas*, St: Martini, Op. I/2, copy British Library (and several other sources).

Modern edition: Bathia Churgin, ed. *The symphonies of G. B. Sammartini. Volume I: The early symphonies.* Harvard publications in music, 2. Cambridge, Mass.: Harvard University Press, 1968. Sym. No. 13.

Orchestral material: For the edition of the symphony made by Newell Jenkins. Zurich: Eulenburg No. 540, 1956.

Recording: Newell Jenkins, conductor, The Italian Chamber Orchestra,

Haydn Society HS 9019 or HSL-74. No other recorded performances are acceptable (as of 1984).

Editorial remarks: The repeats pose a problem in the minuet. Normally, a theme—here the minuet—and its variation would be performed with a repetition of both parts of the movement. This process, however, would greatly lengthen the movement in relation to movements I and III. To this writer, it would be acceptable, therefore, to omit the repeats. Indeed, it would be possible even to omit the movement itself, since it is unlikely that the addition of the minuet is authentic. The variation technique was associated by Sammartini with chamber music—especially the trio sonata—and keyboard music. It occurs in no other movement of the symphonies. The lower parts in the Fonds Blancheton and Simpson print have no indication of the repeat of the minuet for the variation, but it does appear in another printed edition of the trio in E-flat, found in *Sinfonie a due violini e basso dei piu [sic] celebri autori d'Italia* (Paris: Estien, 1747).

Garland Publishing, Inc.   New York & London   1984

Symphony in G major

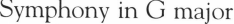

Them. Index J-C 39

Edited by Bathia Churgin

Giovanni Battista Sammartini

I

* m. 14: Quarter rest in the manuscript.

* mm. 23, 24: ♩♪ ?

II

III

IV

Minuetto ($\downarrow$ = *ca.* 108)

Minuetto Variationé

* m. 16: ♩ 𝄾 in all sources, which is appropriate for the variation, but not for the minuet proper.

The Symphony 1720–1840

Barry S. Brook, Editor-in-Chief   Series A-Volume II-Score 4

Symphony in G major
Them. Index J-C 44

Giovanni Battista Sammartini
Milan? 1700 or 1701–1775 Milan

Edited by Bathia Churgin

p. 3 (39)

p. 10 (46)

p. 14 (50)

Instrumentation: 2 violins, viola, bass, 2 trumpets

Date: In the early 1740's, before 1747 (date of Gluck borrowing)

Catalogue references: Breitkopf 1766 (with 2 oboes and 2 horns; attributed to Gluck); Karlsruhe, catalogue E.

Sources used for this edition: Manuscript parts in Karlsruhe, Mus. Hs. 846, "Sonata del Sigr. Giovanni Batta St. Martino," and Prague, Národní muzeum, Waldstein collection XXXIV C 303 (same title as Karlsruhe), both sources Milanese copies by Hand C.

Other sources: (In parts unless otherwise indicated) (1) Zurich, Zentralbibliothek AMG XIII 7043 a–e, Overteur, St. Martino (Milanese copy by Hand B, incipit on title page by Hand C); (2) Dresden, Sächsische Landesbibliothek (a) Musica 2763, N 1, Sonata (Sinfonia on the parts), Martini (with 2 flutes, 2 oboes, 2 horns, bassoon, cembalo), and (b) Sinfonia, St. Martino (score of (a); with 2 oboes and 2 horns); (3) Stockholm, Kungl. Musikaliska Akademiens Bibliotek O-R (Utile Dulci collection), Sinfonia, San Martino (third movement replaced by the longer minuet and trio of J-C 41); (4) Melk, Stiftsbibliothek 1423/V, Sinfonia, St. Martino (with 2 horns; the poorest source); (5) Dresden, Sächsische Landesbibliothek, Musica 3030/F5, movement I only, in score, as the first movement of the overture to Gluck's opera *Le nozze d'Ercole e d'Ebe*, first performed 29 June 1747 in Pillnitz (with 2 oboes and 2 horns); another eighteenth-century score of the opera is in Munich, Bayerische Staatsbibliothek Mus. Mss. 530.

Modern editions: (1) Norbert Zimpel, ed. Zurich: Eulenburg No. 10058, 1973. This is heavily edited and unreliable, as it is based on the Dresden score. (2) Gluck's overture is reprinted in *Denkmäler der Tonkunst in Bayern*, II. Folge, Jg. 14, Bd. 2. The introduction by Hermann Abert includes a reprint of the flute, oboe, and horn parts for J-C 44 in Dresden.

Recording: Newell Jenkins, conductor, Angelicum Orchestra of Milan, Nonesuch H-1162 (mono) or H-71162 (stereo)

Editorial remarks: The Karlsruhe and Prague copies correspond almost exactly in layout and indications. Since the Karlsruhe copy is slightly more accurate, it has served as the primary source, but supplementary markings from Prague (mostly missing articulations, ornaments, and dynamics) have been added whenever necessary without editorial indications. Two different viola parts appear in the sources for movements I and II and are included in this edition for comparison. Viola A, which seems to be the authentic part, appears only in the Milanese copies. It largely doubles the bass at the higher octave and acts as the high bass when the bass proper drops out or merely punctuates. Viola B, found in all the other sources, including Gluck's borrowed movement, is more of a harmonic filler, especially in the first movement. It often settles on the lower strings, particularly in the second movement, producing an uncharacteristic gap between the viola and the second violin. The part was not composed by Gluck, however, whose viola part in the remaining movements of his overture resembles the style of Viola A, being only slightly more independent.

First page of the first violin part for the Symphony in G major (J-C 44) in Hand B; the corresponding page in Hand C is reproduced in the Sammartini thematic catalogue (*Zurich, Zentralbibliothek*)

Garland Publishing, Inc.   New York & London   1984

Symphony in G major

Them. Index J-C 44

Edited by Bathia Churgin

Giovanni Battista Sammartini

I-II

*M. 23, vl I: Same notes as in m. 22 in the basic sources. The text follows vl II.

*M. 27, 29, vl I, II: D tied over the bar line in Dresden (m. 27, 65), Stockholm (m. 29), and Melk (m. 29)

*M. 47, tr: Ties indicated in Dresden score

*M. 51, vl I, II: The upper and lower stems indicate two solutions for note 1. In the basic sources vl I has F♯ and vl II has E. If F♯ is correct, vl II must have D, a note not found in any source. The D♮ chord clashes with vla B, but is the preferable musical effect. If E in vl II is correct, vl II could have G, a note not found in any source. The Zurich copy has E in both vl parts, another possible solution. The Zurich notes appear in Gluck's version, but are preceded by G-F♯ in vl I and E-D♯ in vl II on the last eighths of m. 50, which make parallel fifths with vla A.

*M. 77, tr I: C (concert G) in the basic scores; D (concert A) appears in Stockholm and is preferable.

*M. 79: No tempo mark appears in the sources. In vl I, m. 79¹ and 100¹, and the dotted figures should be coordinated with the triplets in vl II.

*M. 80, vl I: An E♭ appoggiatura appears only in Prague (it is omitted in m. 101).

*M. 82, vl I: Most of the dotted figures are slurred in Zurich, as they would be in performance.

*M. 87–89, vl II: In Prague the slur includes notes 1–4, and the eighth is staccato.

*M. 90, vl I: The trill is found only in Dresden and is implied.

*M. 95–97, vl I: In the basic sources and Zurich copy the bowing here and in m. 105–08 is confused. The slurs as given follow the
    Karlsruhe copy.

*M. 120, 121, tr: In Dresden the rhythm of beat 2 is ♪ ♪.

*M. 120–21, vl I, II: The different bowing from m. 72 to m. 74 seems to be intentional.

III

* **Allegro assai** (♩ = *ca.* 112)

Trombe in G I, II

Violino I Violino II [Unis.]

Viola A–B

Basso

*In the basic sources *Spiritoso* in the vla and b parts, *Allegro* in tr I, II (*Spiritoso assai* in tr II in Prague)

*M. 26, vl I: ♪ in the basic sources. The pattern as given appears in vl II and in all other sources.

*M. 33, vl I, II: Beat 2 is slurred in the basic sources, but the staccatos follow the sequence.

The Symphony 1720–1840
Barry S. Brook, Editor-in-Chief   Series A-Volume II-Score 5

Symphony in G minor
Them. Index J-C 57

Giovanni Battista Sammartini
Milan? 1700 or 1701–1775 Milan

Edited by Bathia Churgin

p. 3 (55)

p. 10 (62)

p. 13 (65)

Instrumentation: 2 violins, viola, bass, 2 horns

Date: In the early 1740's, before 1749 (date of Gluck borrowing)

Catalogue references: Karlsruhe, catalogue A (dated *ca.* 1755–1762); catalogue E.

Sources used for this edition: Manuscript parts in Karlsruhe, Badische Landesbibliothek Mus. Hs. 802, "Overteur del Sigr. Giovanni Batta St. Martino (strings only, source A); and in Prague, Národní muzeum, Waldstein collection XXXIV C 411, "Sonata del Sigr. Giovanni Batta St. Martino" (source A¹), both sources Milanese copies by Hand C.

Other sources: (In parts unless otherwise indicated) (1) Stockholm, Kungl. Musikaliska Akademiens Bibliotek O-R (Utile Dulci collection), Ouverteur, St. Martino (source B); (2) Zurich, Zentralbibliothek AMG XIII 7043 a–e, Sonata, St. Martino (Milanese copy with title page by Hand C; source C); (3) Prague, Národní muzeum, Waldstein collection XXXIV C 319, Overteur, St: Martino; (4) Regensburg, Fürstlich Thurn-und-Taxissche Hofbibliothek, Sammartini 6, Overteur, St: Martino; (5) printed parts of II only, London, A. Hummel, 1761, *VI favourite overtures in six parts . . . composed by . . . Galuppi, St. Martini & Jomelli*, Overture VI/II; (6) Copenhagen, Det Kongelige Bibliotek, 2 copies, Rung C I, 245 and Giedde XI, 12, movement III only, in score as the "Introduzzione" to Part II (strings only) of Gluck's opera *La contesa dei numi*, first performed 9 April 1749 in

Copenhagen; another copy, Berlin, Staatsbibliothek preussischer
Kulturbesitz, Mus. ms. 7787.

Editorial remarks: The sources divide into two groups according to
common variants, the first and preferable version comprising the sources
used for this score and the Stockholm copy. It is possible that this version
embodies revisions of an earlier text preserved in the remaining sources.

First page of the finale, first violin part, for the Symphony in G minor (J-C 57) in Hand C
(*Prague, Národní muzeum, Waldstein collection*)

Garland Publishing, Inc.   New York & London   1984

Symphony in G minor

Them. Index J-C 57

Edited by Bathia Churgin

Giovanni Battista Sammartini

I

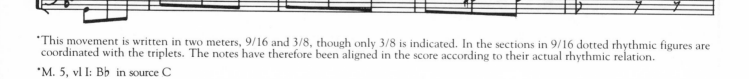

*This movement is written in two meters, 9/16 and 3/8, though only 3/8 is indicated. In the sections in 9/16 dotted rhythmic figures are coordinated with the triplets. The notes have therefore been aligned in the score according to their actual rhythmic relation.

*M. 5, vl I: Bb in source C

*M. 25, cor I, II: D (concert F) in all sources, making a typical clash at the cadence

*M. 32: F in m. 31^t in vl II and vla, sources A, A^1, and B, and in all the strings in source C

*M. 36, vl II: This measure is lacking in sources A and A^1 but appears in the other sources.

*M. 49, 55, vl I, beat 1: Equal sixteenths, staccato, in source C

*M. 51, vl I: A♭ indicated in sources B and C

*M. 60, vl I: Eb-D-C in the sources (wrong notes)

*M. 76, vl I: Staccatos indicated in source C

*M. 93, cor I, II: G (concert B♭) in all the sources, clashing with vl I

*M. 94–95, cor I, II: ♫ ?

*M. 96, vl I: The low G appears in source C.

II

*Upbeat: A sixteenth rest for this figure in the movement, perhaps implying a triplet grouping of the notes that follow, appears in vl I (m. 21), sources A–C, and in vl II, sources A, A¹, C. A thirty-second rest appears in vl II, source B. No triplet sign is found in the sources.

*M. 3, vl II: E♭ in all the sources, clashing with the harmony

*M. 18–20, cor II: The ties appear in source B.

*M. 28, vl II: G in sources A, A¹, B; B♭ in source C

III

*M. 1, 5, vl I, II: The chord includes the low G in sources B and C (except vl II, B, m. 5).

*M. 44, vla, b: C in the vla in sources A–C; C in the b, source C (as well as in m. 42)

*M. 71–74, 79–83, cor II: An octave lower in sources B and C

*M. 83: F, vl I, sources A and A¹ (no marking in source B, and f in m. 84, source C, is clearly a mistake); f in m. 85, vl II, sources A, A¹, C (no marking in B); vla, sources B, C (no marking in A, A¹); and b, sources A–C. The placement in m. 83 is most convincing in relation to the plan of dynamic contrasts in m. 71–92.

*M. 87, vl I, II: A♭ in vl I, sources A, A¹, B; A♮ in vl II sources A–C (and remaining sources). Vl I has F in source C and the remaining sources. The A♭ seems to have been intended for vl II, making a typical cross relation with vl I, beat 3.

*M. 92, vl I: Bowing as in m. 91 in source B

*M. 115, 121, 149, 155, vl I: Slur over notes 1–3 in sources A¹, B, and C (the last only in m. 115)

The Symphony 1720–1840
Barry S. Brook, Editor-in-Chief   Series A-Volume II-Score 6

Symphony in G major
Them. Index J-C 46

Giovanni Battista Sammartini
Milan? 1700 or 1701–1775 Milan

Edited by Bathia Churgin

p. 3 (75)

p. 11 (83)

p. 16 (88)

Instrumentation: 2 violins, viola, bass

Date: On the basis of style, the mid 1740's

Source used for this edition: Manuscript parts in Prague, Národní muzeum, Waldstein collection, XXXIV C 382, "Sinfonia . . . Del Sigr. St: Martino."

Recording: Newell Jenkins, conductor, Orchestra dell'Angelicum di Milano, Disco Angelicum LPA 1701.

Garland Publishing, Inc.   New York & London   1984

First page of the first violin part for the Symphony in G major (J-C 46)
(*Prague, Národní muzeum, Waldstein collection*)

Symphony in G major

Them. Index J-C 46

Edited by Bathia Churgin

Giovanni Battista Sammartini

I

*M. 20, 22, 24, vl I: The dynamics here and in parallel passages are not uniform. In this passage we find *p, f,* and *fp*; in m. 42, 44, and 46, only *fp* in m. 44; in m. 69, 71, and 73, *p, fp,* and *f* (vl II).

*M. 92–93, vl II: Beat 3 repeats beat 2. This passage has been corrected following the parallel passage in m. 29–30.

II

III

*M. 107, vla: E in the MS; either D or F♯ would fit the harmony.

*M. 128, all parts: No *f* indicated until vl II, m. 133

The Symphony 1720–1840

Barry S. Brook, Editor-in-Chief   Series A·Volume II·Score 7

Symphony in C major

Them. Index J-C 4

Giovanni Battista Sammartini

Milan? 1700 or 1701–1775 Milan

Edited by Bathia Churgin

p. 3 (97)

p. 13 (107)

p. 16 (110)

Instrumentation: 2 violins, viola, bass, 2 horns

Date: Before 1760 (Egk catalogue). On the basis of style, *ca.* 1750.

Catalogue references: Egk No. 89, 1760; Breitkopf 1762, Racc. II/2; Karlsruhe catalogue A (*ca.* 1755–1762).

Sources used for this edition: Manuscript parts in Prague, Národní muzeum, Waldstein collection XXXIV C 412, "Sonata del Sigr. Giovanni Batta St. Martino," and Karlsruhe, Badische Landesbibliothek Mus. Hs. 812 (same title as Prague; horn parts missing), both sources Milanese copies by Hand C.

Other sources: (In parts unless otherwise indicated) (1) Venice, Biblioteca del Conservatorio, fondo Carminati-Museo Correr, Busta 9–20, No. 18, Sinfonia, Sammartino (2 trombe da caccia); Vienna, Gesellschaft der Musikfreunde XIII 23566, Sinfonia, St. Martino (with 2 oboes, 2 horns, cembalo; horn and viola parts missing); (3) Stockholm, Kungl. Musikaliska Akademiens Bibliotek O-R (Utile Dulci collection), 3 copies: (a) Sinfonia, Martini, movements I and II (strings only); (b) Sinfonia, anonymous; (c) Sinfonia, anonymous (2 violins and bass only); another copy in the Alströmer collection, Sÿnphonia, Martino; Lund (Sweden), Universitetsbiblioteket Kraus 170, Concerto, Martino (with 2 oboes or flutes, 2 trumpets, timpani), dated 1762.

Modern edition: Ettore Bonelli, ed., Padua: Zanibon, 1956. This is heavily edited and unreliable.

Editorial remarks: The Vienna source is a Breitkopf copy (information from George R. Hill). In Lund, the symphony has four movements, with an additional, spurious Andante in C major. The first and third movements are transposed to D major.

First page of the first violin part for the Symphony in C major (J-C 4) in Hand C
(*Prague, Národní muzeum, Waldstein collection*)

Garland Publishing, Inc.   New York & London   1984

Symphony in C major

Them. Index J-C 4

Edited by Bathia Churgin

Giovanni Battista Sammartini

I

*M. 18, vl I, II, beat 1: In Prague chord lacks bottom G.

*M. 19: *Mf* in vl I and *p* in vla in the basic sources

*M. 30, vl II, vla, b: *P* on first eighth in the basic sources

*M. 62, 63, vl I: No B♭ in the basic sources, though it is needed for the modulation to d minor.

*M. 69, vl I: First note is A in the basic sources.

*M. 104, vl II, vla: *P* on first eighth in the basic sources

*M. 105, vl I: In Prague beat 1 is slurred, and the triplet is B-C-D.

II

Andante e affettuoso (♩ = *ca.* 63)

III

Allegrissimo (♩ = *ca.* 126)

The Symphony 1720–1840
Barry S. Brook, Editor-in-Chief   Series A-Volume II-Score 8

Symphony in A major
Them. Index J-C 62

Giovanni Battista Sammartini
Milan? 1700 or 1701–1775 Milan

Edited by Bathia Churgin

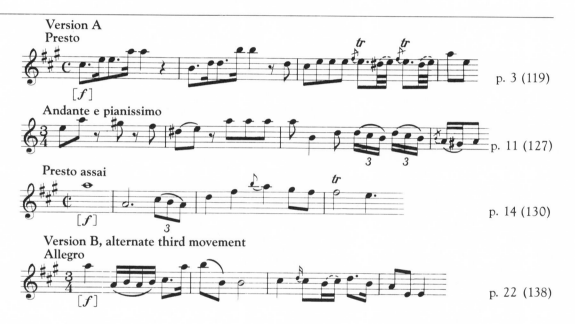

Version A
Presto
[f]
p. 3 (119)

Andante e pianissimo
3 3
p. 11 (127)

Presto assai
tr
[f]
3
p. 14 (130)

Version B, alternate third movement
Allegro
[f]
p. 22 (138)

Instrumentation: 2 violins, viola, bass, 2 trumpets

Date: Before *ca.* 1753–1755 (date of Vernadé-Bayard print). On the basis of style, *ca.* 1750.

Catalogue references: Breitkopf 1762, Racc. II/4; Lambach 1768; Karlsruhe catalogues A (*ca.* 1755–1762) and E.

Sources used for this edition: For J-C 62a: Prague, Národní muzeum, Waldstein collection XXXIV C 299, "Sonata del Sigr. Giovanni Batta St. Martino," a Milanese copy by Hand C (source A); with supplementary indications from Karlsruhe, Badische Landesbibliothek Mus. Hs. 801, "Overteur à più Stromenti Del Sigr. Gio Batta St. Martino," a Milanese copy by Hand B, with incipit on title page by Hand C (source A[1]). For J-C 62b, with minuet finale, Genoa, Biblioteca del Liceo musicale "N. Paganini," N.1.6.6. (Sc. 17), "Overteur Del Sigr. Gio. Batta St. Martino" (with 2 horns), a Milanese copy in the same hand as a copy of J-C 54.

Other sources: (In parts) (1) Stockholm, Kungl. Musikaliska Akademiens Bibliotek, Alströmer collection, Sinfonia, S. Martino (source B); (2) Vienna, Gesellschaft der Musikfreunde XIII 8566, Sinfonia, S. Martino (2 horns; source C); (3) Prague, Národní muzeum, Waldstein collection XXXIV C 387, Sinfonia, St. Martino; (4) Lambach, Stiftsbibliothek, Sinfonia, S. Martino (strings only); (5) printed parts, Paris, Vernadé and Bayard,* ca. 1753–1755; later Venier, ca. 1756–1757, *Sei overture . . . composte da vari autori*, Op. VII/1, Martini (with 2 horns), copy Paris, Bibliothèque Nationale, Conservatoire collection, H. 111.

Modern edition: Walter Lebermann, ed., Mainz: Edition Schott 6176, "Concertino" series, 1970 (for strings only). This is unreliable, with several errors and editorial alterations of the original text.

Recording: Newell Jenkins, conductor, orchestra Accademia dell'Orso, Dover HCR-5247; first recorded on Period SPL 731 (based on the non-Milanese Prague parts (Source 3).

Editorial remarks: Sources 3 and 4 on the list of "Other sources" plus the Genoa source (J-C 62b) constitute a second group of sources, embodying a different, possibly earlier, musical text in certain aspects. The scoring is with horns, and the tempos are *Allegro*, *Andante piano*, and *Presto*. The main differences in the text of the second movement are in vl I: m. 4^1 and 5^1 ♫; m. 4^2 and 5^2, C-natural; m. 8^3, appoggiatura A (to G); m. 25, a different rhythmic pattern, ♪♫ ♩; m. 36^2, D-natural; in vl II: m. 3^1, B eighth and B, C, B, A thirty-seconds; m. 32 note 5, G-sharp. In the third movement, differences occur in vl I: m. 18, the last four notes are eighths; and in m. 20, the notes are B, A-sharp, B, A-sharp, B, G-sharp, E, D. The basic staccato bowing in the first and third movements of J-C 62a is indicated more frequently in the Prague parts. Many additional bowings appear there in the *Andante* in vl I as follows: m. 1^1 and 22^1, slur; m. 2^{2-3} staccato; m. 6^{2-3}, 9^3, 10^3, 23^{2-3}, slurred staccatos; m. 31, m. 34, slur over notes 4–6; m. 32^1, slur over notes 2–4; m. 36, slurs over notes 2–4, 5–8, 9–12.

*The existence and date of the Vernadé-Bayard prints later taken over by Venier as op. 1–8 have been established by Eugene K. Wolf, "On the origins of the Mannheim symphonic style," *Studies in musicology in honor of Otto E. Albrecht*, ed. John Walter Hill (Kassel: Bärenreiter, 1980) 201–04.

Garland Publishing, Inc. New York & London 1984

Symphony in A major

Them. Index J-C 62

Edited by Bathia Churgin

Giovanni Battista Sammartini

I

*M. 16, vl I, II: *F* in m. 15³ in sources A and A¹

II

*M. 8, vl II: F in all the sources, which clashes with vl I. A possible solution retaining F is found in the sources of Group II, where m. 8² has the rhythm ♪♪♪.

*M. 17, vl I: F in sources A, A¹, and B; G, which is more convincing, in source C

IIIa

*M. 10, vl I: Appoggiatura D to C♯ in all the main sources

*M. 31, all parts: No *f* given, though it is implied here and found in the sources of group II.

IIIb

*Minuetto, without tempo mark, in the vla and b

*M. 12, vl I: P on note 1, while in m. 37, p on note 3 (though p on note 2 is most logical).

Symphony in G major
Them. Index J-C 52

Giovanni Battista Sammartini
Milan? 1700 or 1701–1775 Milan

Edited by Bathia Churgin

p. 3 (143)

p. 13 (153)

p. 16 (156)

Instrumentation: 2 violins, viola, bass, 2 oboes(?), 2 horns

Date: Before 1758 (date of Madrid source). On the basis of style, *ca.* 1750–1755.

Catalogue references: Breitkopf 1762, Racc. III/2 (with 2 oboes and 2 horns).

Source used for this edition: Manuscript parts in Prague, Národní muzeum, Waldstein collection XXXIV C 304, "Sonata à più Stromenti Obbligati Del Sigr. Giovanni Batta St. Martino," Milanese copy by Hand C.

Other sources: (In parts) (1) Vienna, Gesellschaft der Musikfreunde XIII 8568, Symphonia, S. Martino; (2) Karlsruhe, Badische Landesbibliothek Mus. Hs. 807, Sinfonia, S. Martino (for strings and 2 trombe da caccia); (3) Madrid, Biblioteca nacional M.2220, Dezima Obertura, San Martino (for strings and 2 horns; viola part only).

Recording: Newell Jenkins, conductor, orchestra Accademia dell'Orso, Dover HCR-5247; first recorded on Period SPL 731 (based on the Karlsruhe copy).

Editorial remarks: For the problem of performance with oboes, see the discussion of the symphony on p. xlix.

Garland Publishing, Inc.   *New York & London*   1984

Title page of the first violin part for the Symphony in G major (J-C 52) in Hand C; the initials
E. W. refer to Emanuel Waldstein (*Prague, Národní muzeum, Waldstein collection*)

First page of the first violin part for the Symphony in G major (J-C 52) in Hand C
(*Prague, Národní muzeum, Waldstein collection*)

Symphony in G major
Them. Index J-C 52

Edited by Bathia Churgin

Giovanni Battista Sammartini

I

*M. 2, vl II: Staccatos from ob II

*M. 2, 64: *P* in vl II and ob II on beats 3 and 2 respectively; in vla on beat 2 only in m. 64

*M. 33, vl I: Slur from ob I

*M. 36–37, 87, vl I: The slurs may have been intended to include notes 1–4.

*M. 44–52: In Karlsruhe, vl I and II have the ob parts of m. 44–47 and 49–52; the vla is given the vl I part, with m. 46–47 and 51–52 an octave lower and m. 49 the same as Prague; the b has the vla part of m. 46–47 and 51–52 an octave lower. M. 48 is the same in the strings as given in Prague. (The vla part in Madrid differs in some details from that in Karlsruhe.)

*M. 76, vl I: The trill appears in ob I in Prague and Vienna.

*M. 81–83, vl I, II: The slurs may have been intended to include notes 1–4.

II

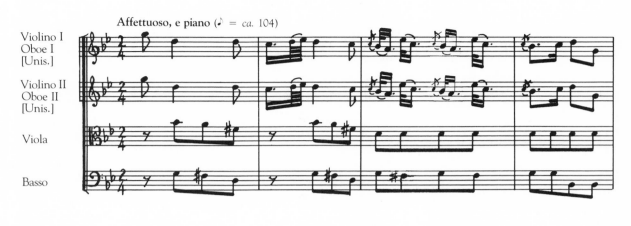

III

*M. 5, 7–8, vl II: Eighth notes staccato (ob II staccato m. 5). In m. 105–08 the parallel measures are staccato in ob II but without markings in vl II.

*M. 53: The clash between the vl I and cor parts seems to be intentional.

*M. 59–60, vl II: Staccatos from ob II

*M. 71–73, vl II: Slurs from ob II

*M. 99, vl II: Staccatos from ob II

*M. 110: Repeat marks for m. 55–110 appear in Prague, vl I, vl II, and b, all parts in Vienna, and vl II in Karlsruhe. However, the marks in the Prague vl parts are in a different hand and were added later. The repeat would unduly lengthen the finale and should not be made.

*M. 111–13, vl II: Staccatos from the Vienna copy

*M. 112, vla: *Pizz.* indication found only in Karlsruhe and implied by the pairing of the vla and b parts

*M. 138, vl I: Slur from ob I

*M. 146: In Prague, ob I has F. If this is correct, vl II must be changed to d¹.

Da capo al segno
% sino al 𝄐

The Symphony 1720–1840

Barry S. Brook, Editor-in-Chief   Series A-Volume II-Score 10

Symphony in E-flat major
Them. Index J-C 26

Giovanni Battista Sammartini
Milan? 1700 or 1701–1775 Milan

Edited by Bathia Churgin

Allegro assai — p. 3 (169)

Allegrino — p. 14 (180)

Allegrissimo — p. 19 (185)

Instrumentation: 2 violins, viola, violoncello, bass, 2 oboes, 2 horns

Date: On the basis of style, the late 1760's or early 1770's (see also next entry)

Source used for this edition: Score in Paris, Bibliothèque Nationale, Conservatoire collection, D. 13. 666, "Sinfonia per Camera Del Signor Gio Batta St. Martino." The score is one of eight scores of Sammartini symphonies made in 1882 for J. B. Weckerlin, librarian of the Paris Conservatoire, from parts formerly in the Conservatoire library and now lost. All the symphonies are late, and seven are unique copies. A twentieth-century score of one of these symphonies, J-C 60, with the same title as the Conservatoire score, has been deposited in the Bibliothèque nationale Vma. ms. 373. Made for Georges de Saint-Foix, pioneer researcher in Sammartini's music, this score includes the date September 1772, suggesting the possibility that all the symphonies scored for Weckerlin stem from around that period, perhaps *ca.* 1768–*ca.* 1774. The homogeneous style of these symphonies supports this dating.

Recording: Newell Jenkins, conductor, Angelicum Orchestra of Milan, Nonesuch H-1162 (mono) or H-71162 (stereo).

Garland Publishing, Inc.   New York & London   1984

First page of the finale, first violin part, for the Symphony in G minor (J-C 57) in Hand C
(*Prague, Národní muzeum, Waldstein collection*)

Symphony in E-flat major

Them. Index J-C 26

Edited by Bathia Churgin

Giovanni Battista Sammartini

I

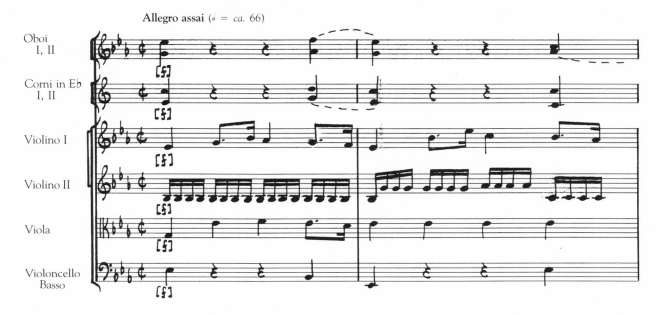

*M. 51–52, vl II: A possible alternate part, following m. 46–47, is indicated in small notes.

II

III

A Note about the Editor

Bathia Churgin is a professor at Bar-Ilan University, Ramat-Gan, Israel, in the Department of Musicology, which she founded and headed from 1970 to 1984. A graduate of Hunter College, she earned her M.A. at Radcliffe College and her Ph.D. at Harvard University in 1963. In addition to having taught for many years at Vassar College, she has been a visiting professor at the Harvard Summer School, Northwestern University, the University of North Carolina at Chapel Hill, Queens College and the Graduate Center, CUNY, Tel Aviv University, and The Hebrew University, Jerusalem. In 1964, she was awarded a research grant by the American Council of Learned Societies. She has specialized in the early Classic symphony, with particular emphasis on the music of G. B. Sammartini and other Italian composers. In her second field of interest, the music of Beethoven, she has produced a new critical edition of Beethoven's Fourth Symphony to be published by Eulenburg.

Author of a dissertation on "The symphonies of G. B. Sammartini," she has published a critical edition of all the early symphonies of Sammartini (Harvard University Press, 1968) and a critical edition, with historical and analytical essays, of Sammartini's late *Sonate a tre stromenti* for strings (University of North Carolina Press, 1981). Churgin is coauthor with Newell Jenkins of the *Thematic catalogue of the works of Giovanni Battista Sammartini: orchestral and vocal music* (Harvard University Press, 1976).